This book is dedicated to the inherent greatness of every child

And to all of you –
Thank you for continuing to shine the light of greatness
upon children everywhere

And thank you for igniting the wildfire of greatness
in this generation and in generations of children to come

ABOUT THE AUTHORS

Howard Glasser, M.A.

Howard Glasser is the founder of Children's Success Foundation and designer of the Nurtured Heart Approach. He and Jennifer Easley are the co-authors of *Transforming the Difficult Child: The Nurtured Heart Approach* (1999), currently the top selling book on the topic of ADHD. He is also the author of *101 Reasons to Avoid Ritalin Like the Plague – Including One Great Reason Why It's Almost ALWAYS Unnecessary* (2005), *The Inner Wealth Initiative* (2007) with Tom Grove, and the *Transforming the Difficult Child Workbook* (2008) with Joann Bowdidge and Lisa Bravo. He has been a featured guest on *CNN* and a consultant on *48 Hours*.

He lectures in the U.S. and internationally, teaching therapists, educators and parents about the Nurtured Heart Approach, which is now being used in hundreds of thousands of homes and classrooms around the world.

Howard is former director and clinical supervisor of the Center for the Difficult Child in Tucson, Arizona. He has been a consultant for numerous psychiatric, judicial and educational programs. Although he has done extensive doctoral work in the fields of Clinical Psychology and Educational Leadership, he feels his own years as a difficult child contributed the most to his understanding of the needs of challenging children and to the success of his approach. He lives in Tucson, Arizona.

Melissa Lynn Block, M.Ed.

Melissa Lynn Block is a writer and editor who specializes in helping others put their brilliant ideas, methods, and stories down on the printed page in the most clear, elegant, and accessible form. Her company, ideokinesis, has clients from many disciplines, including physicians, therapists and educators. She has written, ghostwritten and co-authored more than a dozen books, along with many articles and newsletters and a lot of Web content. She lives with her husband, two children, two stepchildren (part-time), cat, and five chickens in Santa Barbara, California. She can be contacted at idokinesis@verizon.net.

A Note about the Word *Positivity*

Positivity is not an actual word (yet!). But in trying to convey the Nurtured Heart Approach to our readers, we attempted to use other (actual) words and found they either had some interpretive baggage or didn't adequately convey our desired meaning. And since negativity is a word, we felt that it's opposite – positivity – would convey the proper level of vastness we were seeking in our attempts to fully describe the counterpoint of negativity. We therefore took the liberty of "inventing" the word positivity to connote the richest sense of being positive. Again, we hope readers will overlook our incorrectness in this situation and understand our motives.

– Howie and Melissa

ACKNOWLEDGEMENTS

This book is a manifestation of a vision that I've carried and imagined for the past seven years: that the Nurtured Heart Approach is wonderfully suited for all children, not just the challenging children for whom it was originally designed. Still, I am indebted to those difficult children who first inspired the clear and powerful nature of this approach as it came into existence.

I am indebted as well to the many parents and professionals who take this approach into the world each day and who contribute to evolving it into ever-greater levels. Prominent in this group are Tom Grove, Lisa Bravo, and Gabrielli LaChiara, who assist me and lead the way at our Advanced Trainings; and Joann Bowdidge, Jennifer Easley and Jan Hunter, who among the many great therapists and educators certified in this work are major contributors to bringing the Nurtured Heart Approach to the world.

I am indebted to Puran and Susanna Bair for their brilliant Heart-Rhythm Meditation work and for the synergy they have created in our shared interest in igniting the greatness of others.

I am particularly indebted to Melissa Block for her amazing ability to translate my, at times, loosely formed notes and thoughts into a wonderful literary style. What an amazing talent to be able to mold ideas into a complete, coherent, flowing volume, utterly faithful to the author's voice and notions; and to make each and every piece come to life beyond anything I could have accomplished on my own. I am so appreciative of her great skills and attitude. What a gift she is to my life.

I am also greatly indebted to two other people who have made this book come to life. Chris Howell has made a huge contribution to the flow, impact, correctness and readability of *All Children Flourishing* by way of her great and encompassing skills as an editor. Michael Kichler has, once again, magically put all the components into beautiful book form by way of his wonderful talents and skills as a graphic artist.

Last but not least, I want to thank my wonderful daughter Alice for contributing her magnificent and inspiring art for this cover. It brings me so much joy to see the growth between the wonderful artwork she contributed at age seven for the cover of my first book and her great talent now at age 16. I so appreciate of the love and support this amazing child brings to my life.

Howard Glasser

Thanks to Howard for once again giving me the opportunity to contribute to a work that stands to benefit so many, so deeply. The potent combination of his faith in my ability and my respect for his genius seems always to yield something greater than the sum of its parts.

Thanks to all who have supported the evolution of the Nurtured Heart Approach and who continue to tirelessly and joyfully spread the word.

Thanks to editor *extraordinaire* Chris Howell for her invaluable contributions.

Thanks to Susanna and Puran Bair for welcoming me into their retreat in Montecito so that I could experience the interplay of the rhythms of the heart, the breath, and the recognition of greatness. That unforgettable (if too-brief) experience is certain to enrich my future collaborations with Howard.

Thanks to Sumati, Nicola, Nancy and Christine, the powerful women in my life – the ones who remind me of my greatness with reassuring steadfastness.

Thanks to my family: Noah and Sarah for their spectacular everyday wonderfulness; Julian and Tristan, growing up so gracefully; Amanda, my first real parenting guide; and Patrick, who taught me (and continues to teach me) the meaning of intention.

Melissa Lynn Block

TABLE OF CONTENTS

FOREWORD

Written by Puran and Susanna Bair, authors of Energize Your Heart, who teach Heart Rhythm Meditation, a method for connecting the breath with the heartbeat. By manipulating the breath, Heart Rhythm meditators learn to channel energy consciously into the heart – a practice that has turned out to be a natural corollary to the approach described in this book.

In our work, we help others recognize the ways in which the heart affects physical, emotional and spiritual well-being and to access the energy of the heart through meditation. Throughout our most wonderful collaboration with Howard Glasser – contributing to his workshops and enjoying his contributions to the seminars we offer through our Institute for Applied Meditation (IAM) – we have come to recognize that his approach, described in detail in the pages of this book, is a necessary part of opening the heart and revealing a person's true nature.

We teach about the physical level at which the heart communicates with all the organs and cells of the body, directing the organism in the rhythm of health; and about the emotional level, of which the powerful and very sensitive heart is the center. At the spiritual level, the heart holds the light of the soul, like a pond holds the water of the rain, and in this pond one sees reflected the light of greatness. We can find a place of peace in the chaos of life by attuning ourselves to the strength and depth of the heart, and then we can nurture the hearts of our children in ways that help them live from that loving, sensitive and energized place. This is our vision of how to create a more loving world.

In this era of emphasis on the mind, the heart can get ignored. As children are so naturally capable of living from the heart, they also suffer the most from not being able to access their emotions; or if they can access them, from not being able to honor them and harness their power. Their pain at not having their heart's greatness recognized can cause a child to act out, or to become isolated or even self-destructive.

What enables children to live heart-fully and powerfully is adult energy, given in a way that allows them to remember their greatness. When you give the attention and energy of your heart to a child, your every expression is a sincere recognition of the greatness you see right now, right here, in the one in front of you. That energy is received by the other directly into their heart; it is irresistible. The heart is easily wounded but can quickly heal itself when given this kind of attention and energy.

As parents, we hope that our children will know that our words and actions are motivated by love and concern – but they don't; they feel the energy first. The energy *is* the message. We can have an enormous effect on others, our children especially, by the quality and type of energy and attention we give in every moment.

Most people are not used to looking at their actions and words from an energetic point of view, and this is where Howard has made a great contribution – he knows energy. He has created a method for delivering energy from the heart of the parent directly into the heart of the child. The key to this is sincerity; the heart is not fooled by mechanical techniques or artificiality, but it immediately responds to truth. This separates Howard's method from others that are more procedural and rule-bound. You're working here with the energy of love...with true acknowledgement of the greatness of everyone involved in this energetic transaction.

When you feel Howard's admiration of your greatness, you naturally respond like a flower blooming, opening your petals and showing your loveliness. This is love in action, and even the most difficult parts of ourselves are helpless against its transformative power. Not only does Howard have the ability to see greatness in anyone, he treats people with all the respect that greatness deserves. When he points out the ways in which a person is expressing qualities like tolerance, kindness, honesty, self-control, humility, fairness, responsibility and wisdom – and in so doing, is great – he means what he says. His words come from the heart, and that's what makes his Nurtured Heart Approach work.

As you read through this book, you might wonder if one can really live like Howard teaches, acknowledging and supporting the greatness of everyone from friends to supermarket clerks. Does he do this himself? Having worked with Howard, we are delighted to report that he is every bit as sincere in person as he comes across in his workshops and on the pages of his books. He applies his own approach to himself constantly, and he applies it to every person he encounters. Spending time with Howard is a bath in a lovely fountain of the most beautiful qualities of your self. The compliments cascade all around you until you are drenched to the core by his vision of you. You become convinced of your greatness by someone who sees and sincerely believes it.

Simply give your child (or any other person in your life, including yourself) a real compliment, backed up by proof captured in the present moment. You'll first see the smile of someone being "accused of greatness" – and a delighted astonishment at the beauty of the vision of reality you're sharing with them; and then, an inner confidence, dawning as the sun of recognition rises over the dark mountain of self-doubt.

This amazing method of parenting and relationship building is completely focused on the greatness inherent in every human being. It really works. As you read this book, you will find yourself drawn to act in the here and now – to apply the inherent knowledge of your heart to create a more loving world.

Puran and Susanna Bair
The Institute for Applied Meditation, Inc.

INTRODUCTION

Impacting the Life of Every Child

> *There are two ways to live: you can live as if nothing is a*
> *miracle; you can live as if everything is a miracle.*
> – Albert Einstein

This book addresses the use of a specific disciplinary approach –
something I like to call a *curriculum of greatness* – to support and
nourish all children. I call it the Nurtured Heart Approach.

This approach was originally designed to help families help their
"difficult" children better adapt to school and family life. During years
of using this approach with these children, however, I discovered that
it works beautifully to foster inner strength, higher achievement, happiness, security and exemplary conduct in *every child*. It is not just
another "positive" approach to parenting designed to improve behavior. Rather, it's an approach to greatness – a method of recognizing
and appreciating the gifts each child possesses, plus a generous dose
of grace.

Parents who had been desperate to find something that *worked*
and adopted the Nurtured Heart Approach with their difficult child
typically also used the approach with their other children, because it's
just easier that way. They would then report similar, extraordinary
results: they described their other children as *flourishing* beyond anything they had ever seen or experienced before. In other words, the
Nurtured Heart Approach strategies designed specifically for the difficult child work beautifully for the average child.

The techniques need only be applied as intensively as the situation merits. Our rule of thumb over the years has been: **the more intense the child, the more intense the application required.** This
translates into performing the techniques more frequently and with
more detail, intent and emotion with a child who is more "difficult"
or intense.

I have written this book as a companion volume to my first book, *Transforming the Difficult Child,* which I first wrote with fellow therapist Jennifer Easley in 1999. I ultimately felt compelled to write a book that addresses the use of the Nurtured Heart Approach not in a *reactive* way – as a response to unacceptable behaviors or other problems in children – but in a *proactive* way. This approach gives parents enormous power to help *every child* navigate an ever more complex world with confidence and an inner compass of greatness.

Another purpose was to update *Transforming the Difficult Child* to incorporate the invaluable input and support I have gained over the years from those who have attended my trainings and read my books – those who have put the model into practice and have made it their own. They have helped the approach continue to evolve. This volume integrates the progress all of us have made in refining, expanding, and evolving the original approach.

Although I was always pleased about the secondary impact of my work with difficult children on their less difficult peers and siblings, I had resisted the idea of writing a book on this subject. I just didn't see that as my focus; they didn't seem to need as much help as those who were obviously struggling. I was still only passionate about helping difficult children. But this view changed following the infamous day of September 11, 2001.

I now feel an urgency I didn't feel before. I see that children carry more uncertainty and less hope than just a few years ago. They sense the fear of the adults around them. Now, more than ever, children need to be *significantly* stronger on the inside to not only make it, but to make it a better world. They need a real inheritance – not monetary wealth, but *inner wealth.* We may no longer have the luxury of using old methods – traditional ways of instilling self-esteem and enforcing/reinforcing positive choices – considering all that a child faces these days.

We need approaches that put us all in an advantageous situation: a place where parents have tools at their disposal that reliably infuse their children with enormous inner strength. The stakes seem too high to do otherwise. We have to introduce them to who they really are at their core: a child who has and who carries the inspiration of greatness. And I am convinced, now more than ever, that every child has greatness to which they can be introduced if we do it properly.

We can no longer just occasionally urge our children to feel self-worth, to make better choices and to have a better attitude. A more proactive approach is needed. We have to give them incontrovertible evidence, in real time, that they are successful. Note that I'm not talking about their *potential* for success [e.g., "if only he would…(fill in the blank)"]; I'm talking about reflecting to each child that he or she is successful *right now.* This is the foundation that will not only strengthen them enough to weather whatever storms come their way, but also will inspire them to live their lives at an entirely higher and more delightful trajectory.

This approach equips any child to handle difficulties with security and self-confidence; to discriminate between right and wrong; and to ask for and accept any help they may need – all while maintaining their ability to express their individuality and unique strengths.

In some respects, and in some parts of the world, children have more safety and privilege than ever before. But in place of the problems that have been all but eradicated by modern medicine and unprecedented access to education and creature comforts, new issues have arisen.

A large survey by the U.S. Department of Health and Human Services found that in 2002, almost 20 percent of youth aged 12 to 17 received some kind of mental health treatment or counseling; half of them did so because they felt depressed, while another 27 percent did so because of rule-breaking or acting out. Twenty percent of these kids who received mental health services had suicidal thoughts or made suicide attempts; another 20 percent were feeling afraid or tense; and 14 percent had problems with family or at home.[1] Yet another government study reported that six percent of children aged four to 17 were said by a parent to have definite or severe emotional or behavioral difficulties.

---

1 US Department of Health and Human Services, Health Resources and Services Administration, Maternal & Child Health Bureau. *Child Health USA 2004.* Rockville, MD, US Department of Health & Human Services, 2004

Today, government surveys estimate that about 4.4 million children have ADHD (attention deficit/hyperactivity disorder); I have heard estimates as high as 12 million. Another survey estimates that one-tenth of U.S. children have some level of impairment due to mental illness.

Is something wrong with children's brains in the U.S. that isn't affecting other nations – which all have far lower rates of mental health diagnoses and psychiatric medicating in children?

I believe the more likely explanation is this: We have become convinced that inner conflict, spiritual crisis, everyday problems or issues, and clashes between the status quo and those who would like to see it change are actually signs of pathological biochemical imbalances in our brains.

Although this is quite a marketing coup for the pharmaceutical industry, it is a way of looking at children's problems that could ultimately do them great harm. The Nurtured Heart Approach is, at its core, a spiritual solution that strengthens every child on the inside, enabling them to thrive in a way that no medication can.

Take medications away and the next day the child is back to square one, problems front and center, with neither the parent nor the child any wiser about how to fruitfully tap into the child's life force. In contrast, give a parent or teacher an approach that helps every child truly experience their greatness, and it not only persists over time but has a life of its own. The child becomes someone who can channel his intensity to the benefit of self and others.

Some say that the driving force behind rising mental illness diagnoses in children is "increased awareness" of the symptoms and consequences of mental illness. I maintain – based on my own extensive clinical experience and my observations of the many thousands of parents and teachers who have learned and applied the Nurtured Heart Approach – that what is needed by the majority of "diagnosable" children is to have a whole different kind of awareness shone upon them: an awareness of the incredible capacity for success and goodness that exists in every child, *at every moment.*

The Nurtured Heart Approach requires that we, as adults, become aware of that capacity and learn to acknowledge it with strong, inspiring, and truthful language. This kind of acknowledgement is beneficial for every child – whether she is very "difficult," "well-behaved" or somewhere between these two extremes.

Certainly, a "difficult" child struggles more, causes more disruptions in school and at home, and is more challenging to parents. But no child sails through life without problems and conflicts. *Every child* can benefit from an approach to parenting that strengthens them from the inside out. This kind of approach helps children persevere and succeed against the obstacles they will inevitably face – and believe in themselves deeply and completely.

With the Nurtured Heart Approach, we nurture and support children in an all-encompassing, holistic, positive, energized way instead of merely dealing with problems, putting out fires and waiting for the next conflagration. We don't save active, enthusiastic, colorful relationship and recognition of children for those instances when problems arise; instead, we recognize them *when things are going right,* and even better, *when things aren't going wrong.* You will see the beauty of this expanded lens and perspective shortly.

So what about those moments when things are going wrong? In these moments, the approach requires that you *withdraw* your energy, giving the child the perception of having had a consequence – a way of resetting that is brief and un-energized. As you make success irresistible – even inevitable – and negative behaviors less exciting, the child is inexorably drawn to create more success. She begins to believe, in her core, that she possesses greatness – because she has repeatedly been shown, in the moment, the ways in which she is great.

Learning and applying the Nurtured Heart Approach will conflict with most of what you've read about in other books or learned in parenting courses. It will ask you to draw upon your intelligence and creativity to see the world – not just your child – in a new way.

This is not a complicated approach, but it is counter-intuitive. It will call upon you to go against everything you've been taught by your parents and seen other parents do with their children. Just when you would normally feel like giving a long, drawn-out lecture, you'll learn to give a brief reset (or time-out)…and then artistically discern the next moment of success, jumping in to teach the very same "lesson" through positivity. Just when you want to quietly get things done when your child seems to be occupied with a positive activity, you'll learn to take a few moments to creatively, expressively reflect the ways in which the child is being successful. In a way, it will feel as if you're systematically sending e-mails to the child pertaining to his greatness.

You may be skeptical about the power of any time-out/reset – brief or otherwise – to serve as a consequence for poor choices. But it is the power, honesty, consistency, and creativity of your positive acknowledgements that will make the time-out work as a consequence. In this approach, the consequences are absolutely solid, but it is not their severity that leads to the awakening you will see happen in your child. The new and powerful exposure to repeated experiences of success is what will awaken your child to his own greatness.

In Chapters One through Three, I discuss the theoretical underpinnings of the Nurtured Heart Approach. It's important that you read those chapters first, because they will (I hope) drastically change the way you view your child's needs and your role as a parent. Without that paradigm shift, you'll be missing the foundation required to apply what's detailed in Chapters Four through Seven: the nuts and bolts of the approach – everything you need to put the wheels in motion and keep them spinning.

The Nurtured Heart Approach isn't only for children! In Chapter Eight, I share some of my thoughts about the approach through the lifespan – and the ways in which promoting your children's inner wealth will immeasurably enrich your own.

PART ONE: The Paradigm Shift

Greatness lies not in being strong, but in the right using of strength; and strength is not used rightly when it serves only to carry a man above his fellows for his own solitary glory. He is the greatest whose strength carries up the most hearts by the attraction of his own.
– Henry Ward Beecher

Greatness, generally speaking, is an unusual quantity of a usual quality grafted upon a common man.
– William Allen White

CHAPTER ONE

About the Nurtured Heart Approach

> *If one advances confidently in the direction of his dreams, and endeavors to live the life which he has imagined, he will meet with success unexpected in common hours. He will pass an invisible boundary; new, universal, and more liberal laws will begin to establish themselves around and within him; and he will live with the license of a higher order of things.*
> – Henry David Thoreau

> *Divinity is human perfection and humanity is human limitation.*
> – Hazrat Inayat Khan

What would you do if you got to play God for a while?

One of my own answers to that question is that I might arrange for every teacher and every therapist to have their very own biological, foster or adopted challenging child.

I offer this concept not to be mean-spirited – not in the spirit of "You think it's so easy to deal with these issues? Try it yourself!" – but rather as the way to motivate them to practice approaches that would bring all children to the next level of humanity and optimal emotional and psychological health. When your own child is suffering, you're willing to go a distance you might not even begin to grasp when you're working with other people's children.

Having one's very own challenging child might lead these greatly influential people away from the belief that medications are a sensible first resort and toward turning every last stone to find an alternative way to transform challenging children. In finding ways to respond to the challenges of his or her own child, this therapist or educator may find solutions that work for every child and every family encountered in his or her work life.

Or, maybe, if I got to play God, I'd take it one step further: I'd give every teacher, parent and therapist the experience of *being* a challenging child. That's actually how I got into this whole wonderful realm I now inhabit.

Howard Glasser, Difficult Child

Yes, I was what you might call a *difficult child*.

I had intensity to spare, and everyone who knew me found that intensity to be alternately compelling and frightening. As for myself, my own intensity terrified me. Adults made it abundantly clear that this intensity was far from desirable. I was taught to squash it and hide it from view. I was taught to do my best to fit in, to avoid rocking the boat.

As do many difficult children, I entered adulthood with a thoroughly tainted personal portfolio: full of self-doubt, fear, anger and insecurity. I managed to pull myself out of the downward spiral and now enjoy a measure of success and personal happiness.

A big part of this happiness resulted from my work, which is directed toward sparing children what I went through – and sparing adults the difficulties my parents experienced trying to turn a very intense (a.k.a. difficult) child into a productive, contented adult. I knew early on in my work that squashing or mitigating one's own intensity would not be the answer; instead, it would be about embracing it and using it to try to do good in the world.

My parents weren't anything out of the ordinary. They did all they could with the resources they possessed. But the means to direct and cultivate my intensity in ways beneficial to all just didn't exist for them, so they were left simply struggling to control a child who seemed out of control a lot of the time. I'm sure they also spent much of their time hoping, wishing and praying that fate would send my careening ship on a productive and happy course and not into a disastrous storm.

As a child, I believed that people were most interested in me when I was adversarial. That's when people seemed to be willing to drop what they were doing and spend what – ironically – felt like quality time with me. I clearly recall wanting that quality time for just "being me." But if that didn't work, if the only way I could get that juice was through negativity, no problem. I could do negativity.

For every child like me who makes it, there are a hundred who don't: who are tumbled out of childhood into a life that is far from peaceful, happy or productive. I strongly credit grace for enabling me to reach my current place in life. I would define what transpired as a cosmic "time-out" where we get to start over with a clean slate rather than suffering the consequences of past mistakes. Sometimes, as in my case, it just happens – a sort of divine collaboration that sweeps you into a new chance to thrive without the burdens of the past weighing on your shoulders. Unfortunately, it cannot be relied upon; its nature is such that it doesn't always show up when needed, and when it does, we don't always take advantage of it. I clarify this point because the "time-out" – a new kind of time-out, which will be described in detail later on – is an important part of the Nurtured Heart Approach. By learning to use this tool with your child, you will learn how to invoke grace in your life and your child's in a perfectly orchestrated way. Again and again, grace-fully, you let go of the previous moment and return to the present moment, in all its shining glory.

Having been a difficult child, I was drawn to help others like myself. As you already know, the approach I developed – or, rather, that developed me – is called the Nurtured Heart Approach.

An Approach Is Born

My training as a therapist, which consisted mostly of working with adults, did not adequately prepare me for the work I took on later in life with children and their families.

Although I had acquired many viable skills along the way that worked consistently well with adults – how to help people communicate better with others; to constructively feel and express their innermost feelings; or to use cognitive and rational approaches to problem solving – *these same skills,* when applied to challenging children and their families, seemed to make their situations worse, not better. And the harder I tried to help these children and families by using these traditional techniques and recommendations that, by all accounts, *should* have worked, the worse the situation became.

It was a rude awakening.

At the time, I was working in the juvenile court system, in what's called a diversion program: a last-ditch effort to keep kids who had been arrested out of jail. Parents were often furious with their child and often furious with themselves for not having kept their child out of trouble. They knew they were being looked upon as dysfunctional parents who had not done their jobs. I must have worked with a thousand of these parents, but one stands out in my memory. Like the others, he had begun to think of himself as a bad parent.

David was a brilliant scientist – not nerdy at all, but funny and interesting. His son had lived with his mom for a time, then had come back to live with dad and had gotten in some serious trouble. David had read every parenting book and tried as hard as he could to help his son. If this well-read, smart, loving father couldn't figure out how to keep his son from committing crimes, I realized that there must be something wrong with the methods we were using.

In the long run, these challenges became a great asset. As I gave up on "normal" approaches and allowed my inner guidance to direct my recommendations to clients, especially in light of my own extensive personal experience as a challenging child, an approach emerged.

At the time, however, I was thoroughly frustrated with my ineffectiveness at helping these children and families and was tempted to throw in the towel and go back to working with adults and therapeutic milieus, fields in which I had experienced a good deal of success in prior years.

But then I had a series of epiphanies that inspired me to stick with my work with children. These epiphanies changed my life dramatically and led to the birth of my approach.

I began to experience what felt like full molecular, cellular, nuclear memories of my own difficult childhood. In my bones, I could feel all the memories and sensations of being a difficult child myself, feelings I had tried to forget, especially in relation to family dynamics. Being in the room with these families allowed me the gift of feeling the situation at an energetic, almost electro-magnetic level, in an utterly physical way. And it was as if my heart was the central receptor of this revealed truth. I felt like I might be going a little crazy.

It seemed I couldn't quiet down even for a minute without my internal message service sounding the bell that I had "mail" (more sensations, recollections and strange ideas). Call it what you want: intuition, channeling, transmissions from another planet. Wherever they came from, these ideas seemed…well, *silly*. I couldn't seem to rid myself of these ridiculous notions that were flooding my life.

Eventually, out of a blend of curiosity and frustration, I started to bring pieces of these silly notions and ideas into my work with difficult children and their families. And I was consistently floored by the immediate positive response I saw in the adults and their children. I began to recognize that these notions weren't so silly after all; they were, in fact, *intentions* that helped parents make an important paradigm shift.

These ideas appeared to grab the parents I worked with in a novel way. I could see them saying to themselves, "YES, that makes total sense!" Time and again, these ideas created experiences so powerful that my clients couldn't seem to wait to put them into motion.

These notions or ideas, tested with families of difficult children, eventually evolved into the Nurtured Heart Approach, which you will learn about in this book. As my successes with the approach grew, it was not unusual to get calls asking if I could take on yet another *very challenging* case. All of a sudden, referral sources were sending me their toughest cases: kids who were using drugs, kids in out-of-home placements, kids who were suicidal, kids who were runaways, and kids who had joined gangs, along with lots of kids who were simply out of control.

Looking back, I can see that these greater challenges forced me to rapidly evolve the emerging approach. My only other choice was to write these children off because they didn't respond to the existing approaches that their parents and teachers were already using. I wasn't willing to do that.

As I refined and experimented with the approach, it proved to have significant positive results in even the toughest cases. I had yet to discover its impact on all children.

A Serendipitous Finding

The stories of "normal" children who were inadvertently exposed to this approach trickled in at first. Soon I was flooded with reports of the extraordinary effects it was having on less difficult or intense children in families and classrooms. The word "flourishing" often was used to describe these effects.

The dictionary defines *flourishing* as "growing vigorously; thriving; prosperous." This is a perfect word for our purposes, as this is exactly what we want to see in any child: vigorous growth, continual accruing of inner wealth, and general ability to thrive in whatever circumstances he or she encounters.

In the old days, when I studied psychology, all my notions were very complex. As I've matured in my thinking, I find that the notions I have to offer are becoming increasingly simple. The simpler the ideas get, the more readily and easily people are able to run with them – so I've become extremely fond of simple!

I soon had to recognize that these "loco notions" – the simple intentions I was developing and applying in therapy – would prove helpful for all children.

The Original "Silly Notion":
Parents Are Their Children's Favorite Toys

As I began to integrate my intuitions about difficult children into my therapy practice, I started to give parents a spiel that went something like this:

Think about your child with a new toy. He's likely to spend time exploring all it has to offer – checking it out, experiencing all the toy's responses to his manipulations. The typical toy has features, and whether there are two, 10 or 100, some will be more exciting and engaging than others. Hopefully, some will be compelling, and if so, those are the features your child will return to over and over again.

Imagine how your child tends to go back to a boring feature to see if it might change. Once he determines that it is truly and predictably boring, doesn't he write it off and refuse to interact with that aspect of the toy?

Now, think of us adults as toys for a few seconds. How many features do we have as human beings? Even someone who is physically handicapped has virtually unlimited nuances of movement, expression, mood and emotion. We have practically limitless ways we can respond, connect and demonstrate closeness and animation.

An adult is, for all intents and purposes, the ultimate toy.

(Invariably, I'd see the parents' faces light up with recognition here.)

I would then explain:

*Just by watching and experiencing life, children drink in impressions from day one about how the world works. Many children – particularly those who are more needy, intense and/or sensitive than the next child – form their impressions in a specific way that leads to challenging behavior issues later on...because **they see that the adults in their lives, their ultimate toys, are much more interesting when things are going wrong than when they are going right.** We adults have far more captivating, energized, animated responses to children when there is adversity. And the traditional or conventional approaches to parenting merely reinforce this impression.*

Then we would examine the specific "features" of the parent as toy:

Adults tend to be more tuned-in when things are going wrong. Adversity inspires adults to "launch their software" with more emotion, discussion, relationship, intimacy and presence.

Think about it, and ask yourself what really makes your features pop. Is it when your child says "no" to doing what he's told? When she leaves her room a mess? When he underachieves at school? When she snaps back at you with sarcasm or disrespect?

Think about how you respond when your child pushes your buttons and you'll realize you probably get quite animated. Perhaps your voice gets louder and more expressive, your body gets active or you get physically close to your child in your attempt to deal with what you see as a problem behavior.

While you might consider this to be a punishment or something to be feared on the part of your child, he may not view it that way at all. He might dislike that you are angry with him or lecturing him, but energetically, he's being fed in a way he rarely is when he's doing all the right things. He makes a great discovery: "I can really make this toy "pop" just by breaking the rules!"

When things are going well – when the child isn't having issues or problems – we, the toys, are relatively boring. We tend to have relatively little presence, not much to say and don't tend to give much energy to what we do say. And, as with the boring features of a real toy, the child will likely write us off when this is the response typically accorded when things are going well.

The child therefore is more likely to attach herself with greater determination to the features that tap into the mother lode: greater levels of presence. *Doesn't your child go for the feature of a toy that makes the most noise or that creates the most movement or spectacle... that strikes her as most exciting?*

When I presented this notion of parents as favorite toys to the parents of the children I was charged with helping as a therapist all those years ago, they recognized, just as you may have in these past few moments, that they were accidentally rewarding their children for poor choices.

At their core, children want adult presence and energy. Some children need bigger, more powerful doses than others; generally, unless they've given up on us, the more connection they can get with us, the better. The intense child needs this so much that he wants the most rapid, sure-fire route for obtaining it from his favorite toy; he soon discovers this juicier connection is so much more consistently available through the creation of conflict, chaos and disruption.

Less intense or difficult children need adult presence and energy, too, but may be less likely to "go for it" with the same lawless gusto. They may pine for it, only to receive it when they accomplish something good enough to get them noticed. There certainly are children who don't exhibit any outward signs of behavior issues but who silently suffer the lack of adult presence and energy, not knowing how to consistently elicit it from the adults in their lives.

The average child might see the negative responses of an adult toward adversity as enough of a deterrent to stop pushing those buttons. But with the typical "difficult" child, *the need for the figurative bells, whistles and flashing lights from their favorite toy is greater than their need for approval.* They can get all those features going like gangbusters...they know exactly how to do it. They aren't *trying* to drive you crazy; rather, they are drawn, almost magnetically, to the greater, more intriguing level of response.

As I continued to channel these notions through myself and out to parents of difficult children, I began to realize that there are two sides to this, as to any, coin. On one side, we need to reverse the flow of energy, presence and recognition, offering it *when things are going right and not when things are going wrong.* As a result, the features of the adult "toy" that are displayed when the child is doing the right things suddenly become much more engaging. (And we certainly can vastly expand the concept of "when things are going right" as you will soon see.)

Here is the other side of the coin: If we fail to balance this shift in energy, recognition and presence by *withdrawing* energy and focus in response to negative behaviors, we undermine our own efforts.

As we "de-energize" our responses to limit-pushing and rule-breaking, we change the features of the parental toy. Instead of lighting up and making noise in response to problem behavior, we do so in response to the lack of problem behavior. After a period of getting reoriented to this "new" feature, the child will seek out the newly exciting responses he gets when he's being "good." And this, as you'll see, quickly leads to "great." This two-sided coin is the basic foundation of the Nurtured Heart Approach.

This may sound strikingly similar to the widespread practice of trying to "catch the child being good" and then giving rewards in those moments. However, the whole traditional notion of "being good" won't suffice for this approach. Nor are we able to bring about transformation unless we have what amounts to a perfect level of limit setting. It is the combination of all these elements that really brings about inner wealth and helps all children flourish.

A New Take on "Being Good"
No longer will you wait around to "catch the child being good." That's like trying to catch a dinosaur in a butterfly net. It's too limiting. In order to cultivate the inner wealth of a child, we need to expand our vision of "creating" goodness – actually *greatness,* which is a whole other galaxy – so that this proverbial net fills the room, the house, the entire world of the child. We make success *unavoidable* for the

child and then feed his need for recognition with abundance and precision.

There's no escape. We hijack the child into success! We soar beyond goodness…and pass into another dimension: greatness.

On Greatness

> *Those who really seek the path to Enlightenment dictate terms to their mind. Then they proceed with strong determination.*
> – Buddha

This book is really, at its core, about manifesting greatness. It gives you tools with which to help your children's greatness shine forth, creating abundant inner wealth.

Participants often come in at the start of my workshops barely possessing the ability to appreciate themselves for being good. In time, they begin to spot the glimmer of their own greatness as well as that of others. It's a dimension that is always there and needs only to be recognized to shine forth brilliantly. The joy I feel upon witnessing this kind of transformation never fades. And when this passage into greatness is witnessed by other participants, the joy of all present is palpable.

Greatness is about staying in the NOW, rather than in the past and the future, and capturing the greatness inherent in this very moment. As parents, we can capture the greatness manifested by our children in each moment, just as a camera captures an image. Greatness can build like an avalanche that becomes a permanent mindset/"heart-set" within the child.

As any individual – parent or child – assimilates a core sense of greatness, it becomes their essence, their reality: *who they really are.*

If your inheritance from childhood was an undoubting, confident sense of yourself as a person who lives strong values, chances are good that you are living a life of greatness. This does not necessarily mean that you are the president of a university or have some other career of great impact – but it does mean that you are having a positive influence on those you encounter.

A life of greatness means consistently making choices that enhance rather than hurt your relationships and endeavors. A life integrated with greatness is more likely to be endowed with inner wealth. It enables one to be in touch with, pursuing and living one's dreams, rather than being frightened by them or stuck in other ways.

So many cultures and faiths profess some version of the phrase "God is great." People pray to God for love, mercy and compassion. Prayer and praise are two sides of the same coin. If you are made in the image of God, you praise that power when you praise yourself and your children. Bringing forth our own greatness – God's creations finding the greatness in themselves – could be exactly what pleases God the most.

Many of us have no trouble attributing greatness to God, or Spirit, or the powers that drive our universe. Many of us have no trouble attributing greatness to people we admire. Why not to our children? Why not to ourselves?

If you are not a religious person or a believer in a monotheistic God, you can find similar teachings in other faiths and other realms. In becoming aware of the amazing mystery that is our world, and in opening to its greatness, you will naturally see that greatness reflected in the people in your life. Creating greatness in the world of your child is a function of knowing it's always there for the picking, like a bountiful grove of fruit, and reflecting it with fierce power and commitment. And it can be done now, no matter where you were yesterday or even before this very moment in which you are reading these words.

The Nurtured Heart Approach is like a voice-over to any frame we select in the movie of our lives. You are in control of that voice-over. Knowing, seeing and speaking greatness is your choice. We have much to be grateful for – but also, we have every reason to be great-full! See the difference? See the similarity?

Gretta

Gretta is a lively, bright, friendly 7-year-old who is usually agreeable. However, like most children, she has her moments.
In those moments – usually where limits are being hotly

contested – she can fire off words and actions that rock the walls at home and turn all heads when out in public.

Once her mother learned the Nurtured Heart Approach, she chose to purposely "create" successes at times when the arguments weren't happening. These times became windows of opportunity to deliver messages of gratitude to Gretta for her willingness to avoid poor choices. Gretta's mother went even further by choosing to identify Gretta's actions as aspects of her greatness.

For example: "Gretta, you looked like you thought about fussing when I said no to a snack, but you didn't. Right now, you are choosing not to argue and I am very grateful. You are being thoughtful and considerate and those are great qualities and great choices you are making."

Can a 7-year-old hear statements like this? Absolutely – a lot better than the long-winded attempts to reason with her during a tirade!

Gretta no longer argues. She has developed tremendous inner strength and ability to use her passion in intensely wonderful ways.

Warrior Thinking: Annihilating Negativity with Greatness
This approach isn't a "wishy-washy-gramma's-love-here-quit-crying-have-a-cookie-and-watch-some-TV" approach. It doesn't encourage victim thinking ("Oh, poor child, he's had such a hard life, who could expect him to do well?") or pathology thinking ("She's ADHD so she can't be expected to succeed"). In contrast, I describe it as a *fierce* approach. We nurture, yes, but we do it like warriors, with strong, focused intention and unswayable purpose. The intensity of this approach is one of the elements that makes it work so well for children who are intense themselves.

One evening, I was dining with some friends who had seen me communicating this sense of greatness to the troubled grown son of another friend. The friends I was dining with told me how impressed they were with the way in which I made greatness an inescapable realm for that young man. I found myself saying, a bit brazenly perhaps, that I could "annihilate him with greatness!" Thinking on that afterward, I found myself cringing a little; but the more I considered it, the more sense it made.

By using the word "annihilate" with regard to this young man, I meant that I can destroy the old self that believes it is inadequate, a failure, nothing but trouble, worth little or no love, and anything *but* great…and essentially replace it with a new self that believes in its own greatness as strongly as it believes the sun will rise every morning.

As a parent who is determined to take your child to that place, think of yourself as a warrior. If your powerful intention is to shine light on your child's greatness, no one can stop you. It's a done deal.

In my work with children, I am always utterly honest in how I interpret the moment and reflect it back to the child. **BUT: I am not going to play fair. It's not going to be a level playing field.** I'm going to win the war of convincing the child that he is successful. It's virtually inconceivable that he will remain tied to his existing belief that he is unworthy. I will triumph in convincing him that he is great! If I win, the child ultimately wins.

From this point on, you can consider yourself a spiritual warrior whose mission is to help your children grow into greatness. In this quest, you will find yourself growing in that direction as well.

Beyond "Good Job" and "Thank You"

All this is accomplished quite simply: by adults choosing to supply major energy to their children's choices to *not* break the rules and their other good decisions that promote cooperation, care, learning and positive relationship.

Instead of adults firing off tired, under-energized, vague statements like "good job" and "thank you," they make more elaborate statements of appreciation and recognition from the heart – **external** statements that lead a child to a first-hand **internal** experience of success.

In my development of this approach, and with the helpful feedback and collaboration of the many individuals I've trained in its use, I have cultivated some specific language that works really well for this purpose. A big part of learning the Nurtured Heart Approach is learning how to use this language and how to speak it in a way that comes from your own heart, with your own original touches.

Much of this book is devoted to detailed explanations of this kind of language – the heartfelt use of which relies on your willingness to perceive your child's actions and behaviors in a new and inescapably positive light.

The Word Gets Out
Even when the Nurtured Heart Approach was just beginning to take shape, it became obvious that the underlying intentions and ideas were providing an effective foundation for children who had seemed beyond help. In Tucson, where I live and work, no one else seemed to be getting results with these children, and when I did, people wanted to know what I was doing. Initially, I refused to tell them, for two reasons: First, because I thought that these strategies that had emanated from my innermost being were just too idiosyncratic, perhaps even too strange; and second, because I hated public speaking. I felt there was no way to even begin to coherently explain what I was doing in a way that other professionals would understand.

I was terrified that the concepts and practices I was developing, and with which I was getting greater and greater results, would get me laughed out of the therapeutic community. Still, as it all continued to "cook" together and become a cohesive approach yielding miraculous outcomes, word got out, and I got more challenging cases. These challenges helped me a great deal to bring the approach to more powerful levels.

Eventually, my arm was twisted by an agency to which I was indebted. I agreed to do an in-service – and hated it. I promised myself I would never do it again. But then, two months later, I was approached in the grocery store by a man who had heard my talk. He turned out to be the supervisor of 10 counselors in the family preservation unit at the agency where I had spoken. (The family preservation unit is the one that deals with consistently challenging children and situations.) Most of his counselors, he told me, were already using this approach exclusively, with great results.

Apparently, there was no turning back.

Spreading the Word

As I refined the approach, I found that successfully treating children with symptoms comprising the syndrome referred to as Attention Deficit Hyperactivity Disorder (ADHD) was – if you can believe this – a piece of cake. I found a way to shift an intense child with hyperactive symptoms to one who uses that intensity beautifully, typically in the course of less than a month.

My colleagues were incredulous; they believed that this syndrome was actually very difficult to treat and that it most often required the use of one or more medications. It was clear, however, that I was getting results. As a practicing therapist, I found myself receiving referrals of ever more difficult cases – children who did not respond to the standard behavior modification approaches commonly used in those cases. It quickly became obvious to me that intense, difficult children could thrive with an approach tailored to work with their intensity and not against it.

Soon, I began teaching the approach in schools to counselors, teachers and administrators. Naturally, they wanted to learn how to apply the approach with children whose behaviors were disruptive. But I soon realized that selective use of this approach **had detrimental effects** on other students – particularly marginal students who were hovering on the borderline between good and bad choices. These students saw the "bad" kids getting a kind of attention that any child would crave, and some went after it by changing their behaviors for the worse. Others who were not willing to go that far sat on the sidelines feeling left out and resentful.

I also began hearing statements such as these over and over from parents: "Thank you for the approach. It's made a world of difference with my difficult child…*AND a world of difference for my other children.* They are *all* flourishing well beyond anything in the past, and I know it's what *I'm* doing that is making the difference." Similar statements came from teachers who were able to transform troubled classrooms into places where learning could happen far more smoothly.

It filled me with joy to hear that so-called "normal" siblings of difficult children were reaping huge benefits from the parents' use of the Nurtured Heart Approach. This information also helped me see the reason that, in a classroom setting, teachers who applied this approach only for a select few difficult children did not have success.

In most schools, there's one child who comes to "rule the school." One example that comes to mind is a boy named (ironically enough) Kane. He was a pleasure to have around...until he got frustrated, which he often did in school due to a learning disability. When this happened, he could completely disrupt a classroom in no time flat.

In response to any inkling of unfairness, he would quickly escalate from calm to hysterical; he would clench his fists, his face would turn red, and he would begin to scream and shout. After he calmed down, he always felt terrible and claimed he could not control his temper. He was losing friends and racking up ever-escalating consequences for rules broken during these bouts of temper. (Trying to enforce those consequences would often lead to another bout.) He was thought of around the school as a problem kid.

Kane was a child who inspired the school counselor, Karen Jennings, to investigate the Nurtured Heart Approach. She had great success with Kane – and soon found that it enormously helped every child who was exposed to it. This is the beauty of the difficult child in each classroom: He or she can guide everyone to higher-order solutions. Because of Kane's fits of temper, every child in that school is now prospering in a whole new way.

With this approach, the best results come from its use on every child. I started to actually refuse to teach it to teachers who wanted only to use it with challenging children. It became increasingly clear that this is an "all or nothing" proposition.

Besides: every kid has his or her moments. It's not unusual for normal kids to occasionally build up a head of steam. Those problems can disrupt family life, school or belief in self. They can set the stage for mistakes that can have terrible consequences. Any parent who's been there knows that even a "good child" can go from zero to 60 into problems. When this happens, parents can feel helpless to guide that child, once so well-behaved, to a better place. This is one reason why this approach, initially designed for "difficult children," has a place in any household, in any school.

One parent told me that her child, once so easygoing and obedient, was suddenly "freaking out" from anxiety. Nothing had changed in their family's routine. Something in her seemed to snap, and she was suddenly afraid of all kinds of things: going to bed, going to school, singing in her church choir, talking on the phone. She thought her friends no longer liked her. She was constantly asking questions about her own health, worried that a rash or pain was a serious disease and asking to be taken to the doctor. The child's intensity was spiking. She was having a spiritual crisis and needed a lot of support. She became "difficult."

My point here is that there's often no clear delineation between a *difficult* child and a *normal* child. Why not apply the same techniques to all children, as long as they serve as beneficial?

The Tale of Tolson Elementary
Tolson Elementary School in Tucson, Arizona, was the first school to take on the Nurtured Heart Approach school-wide. Their results over the past seven-plus years have been awe-inspiring.

Principal Maria Figueroa realized it was not the *academic* curriculum, but the *social* curriculum, that was driving suspensions, teacher burnout, classroom problems, academic failure, mental heath referrals and medication referrals in schools. She realized that the Nurtured Heart Approach was a way to deliver a social curriculum with messages of value, competence, respect and belonging. She has made her vision a reality for thousands of students.

Tolson is a school of more than 500 students, over 80 percent of whom qualify for free and reduced lunch programs because they are largely disadvantaged children, many dealing with poverty, family stresses and limited access to health care resources. This school once had the highest rate of suspensions in a district of over 60 schools: eight percent of the total number of students suspended in the district. (Across-the-board averages would predict that Tolson should experience less than two percent of total district suspensions.)

In 1999, the Nurtured Heart Approach was implemented school-wide. Since that time, Tolson has had only two suspensions (the same student, twice); no referrals to the juvenile justice system; no bullying; dramatic decreases in referrals for special education; no referrals for ADHD evaluations; and no new children on ADHD medications.

Expenditures on special educational services have dropped dramatically in this school, from providing services for nearly 15 percent of students to a current level of under 2 percent. Teacher attrition, which had been over 50 percent annually, evolved to *zero* for three years. Tolson's standardized test scores also have risen considerably since this approach was implemented. Dr. Figueroa is fond of saying that, although the faculty prizes and encourages academic accomplishment, they do not teach to the test. They do, however, teach to each child's greatness.

As children drink in the truth of their greatness, they manifest it in wider and wider circles of endeavor. Children who begin to feel great about themselves want to do their assignments, want to participate, want to be tuned in and want to be prepared. You no longer have to twist their arms. They want to do well on their tests, regardless of pressures or situations in their lives.

Certainly this school still gets at least its fair share of children at risk. Its classrooms are still largely populated by students in low socioeconomic brackets and belonging to minorities traditionally at greater risk of underachievement and behavior problems. But the school is now wired to propel these children toward their destinies of greatness.

So inspiring to me were the transformations I saw at Tolson that I formed the Children's Success Foundation, which has the mission of bringing the Nurtured Heart Approach to educational communities. Since that time, many educators have attended trainings, and many others have implemented the approach by reading my books and taking the leap.

At this writing, nearly 20,000 people have attended my workshops; almost 100,000 of my books have been purchased. It seems that this approach is finding its way, surely and steadily, to those who need it. It is finding its way into schools all over the country. As parents see their children doing so much better in those schools, they want to know more about the approach being used, leading more parents to try the model at home.

In 2007, I published *The Inner Wealth Initiative*, a book on the use of the approach in schools, which I authored with Tom Grove (a therapist who specializes in teaching the Nurtured Heart Approach to educators) and writer Melissa Lynn Block.

My belief is that increased use of this model in schools will yield improved test scores and dramatic decreases in medication use and ADHD diagnosis. I also believe that it will greatly diminish the number of children diagnosed with disorders related to anxiety and depression, while cutting teacher attrition and special education services. I predict that schools where the approach is used will see higher rates of college entrance. Districts will save enormous financial resources: When a district of 10,000 children drops from 15 percent utilization of special education services to even 10 percent, three million dollars can be saved each year. At Tolson, utilization of special education services dropped from 15 percent to 1.2 percent! And better yet, the population enrolled in the school's Gifted and Talented Program rose from less than 2 percent to 15 percent. Now *that's* a true expression of "no child left behind."

Other Potential Positive Effects of the Nurtured Heart Approach

We can go well beyond improvements to transformation, where children find their greatness while they are still young. They won't have to go on a mad search for it in their adult years like so many of us had to do. Our transformed, flourishing youth won't have a legacy of believing that the best way to achieve presence with self or others is through negativity. Rather, they will stand a great chance of truly enjoying people and life itself in a straightforward, congruent way.

I also believe that increased use of this approach in schools will significantly reduce drop-out rates, cigarette, alcohol, and drug use, and teen pregnancy.

In my home state of Arizona, as in most other states, a variety of programs exist to educate children about the risks of drugs. Many of these programs use role playing to help children cope with situations that they're likely to encounter. That format has its merits, but show me a child who has passed that program with flying colors but has *not yet* become strong enough on the inside, and I'll show you a child who is still likely to say *yes* to peer pressure and temptation. That child will remain in a compromised position, unable to conjure up her wherewithal when it is needed the most. In contrast, show me a child who is strong on the inside, and who has yet to go through drug abstinence education, and I'll show you a child who is far more likely to "just say no" out of inner strength and self-love, no matter how intense the pressure from peers. It may still be a struggle for that child, but her strength and power give her the inner resources to make the right choices. This approach is designed specifically to create those inner resources in every child.

You can begin using this approach with any child, very early in that child's life or anytime thereafter. My own daughter has been raised with this model since birth, and as a young woman, she enjoys a level of inner wealth, peace and confidence that makes my heart sing. When you apply the approach to all of your children, you'll see what should be meant by the phrase "no child left behind."

I hope that your interest is piqued at this point; you know that this approach produces results both with difficult and with "normal" children and helps whole schools succeed. You may be asking yourself: How can one approach be so powerful? In the next chapters, you will learn the foundations of the Nurtured Heart Approach – foundations that began with my original notions and intentions all those years ago that have been tested, tried and refined in the laboratory of the real world in which we and our children live.

Let's move on to those concepts that will create your new "toolbox" as a parent who wants to help all your children flourish.

CHAPTER TWO

The Right Tools for the Job

For most of the history of our species, parenting has been a practice directed by a combination of intuition, instinct and customs of the cultures within which we live. Today, most new parents are offered countless theories, techniques and directives about parenting, many of which do not work seamlessly with one another – and may even conflict.

Many parenting partners come from distinctly different cultures with incongruent expectations about parenting and children's behavior, which can be a huge source of marital strife. They choose this approach or that one, or pieces of several, as they grasp for what works to accomplish their parental goals and manage the everyday demands of life with children on this planet. When one approach doesn't work, they read something suggesting a different approach, and change and inconsistency rule the day.

Many of us are doggedly trying to raise our children *differently* than we ourselves were raised, and advice from our parents or grandparents runs counter to our own ideas about what's best. Our parental "toolboxes" can turn into a jumble of tools that don't work smoothly with one another.

And because we have so many choices in terms of how we approach parenting, we often end up blaming ourselves when we make choices as parents that seem to hurt more than they help.

With some children, no matter how badly we screw up as parents, they'll come through just fine; grace has endowed them with some fount of inner strength that enables them to thrive despite all odds. With other children – really, *most* children – a parent's approach can make all the difference.

The flip side of this is the question of blame. If we hold the power to guide our children into making the choices that will ultimately benefit them, does our failure to guide them in that direction mean that we are to blame for their issues and problems? In a word: No.

The Blame Game

Like so many therapists, I was trained in a blend of theory and practice that inherently implied that parents were to blame for any problematic issues encountered by the child. Not many professors intended to come across that way, but the strong implication across society has long been that, if a child is not doing well, some level of dysfunction must be occurring in the family. Any set of parents with a child with behavioral problems has been given the message, from some source or another, that they are the culprits.

No matter how sensitively a school informs a parent that her child has issues, that parent is not about to walk out of that meeting singing happy tunes. To the contrary, the parent may well feel as though she has been blamed and is expected to change things, *pronto*.

Parenting is a huge part of who we are. A parent whose parenting abilities have been called into doubt can feel like a great big hole has been punched right through him. That parent will want to go to whatever lengths are necessary to prove himself or herself able to rectify whatever problems are coming up for the child.

When things are not going well with your child, not only are you faced with the daily struggle to maintain an orderly, safe, peaceful and enriching home environment for your family (along with preserving what's left of your own sanity), but you also know that everyone from therapists to teachers to grandparents to folks on the street tend to place blame on the parent when they see a parent struggling with a child who is misbehaving. You may even know from having on occasion blamed *other* parents for their own child's untoward behaviors. "Why doesn't that parent just...(fill in the blank with your most-heard or most-offered piece of advice)." Even if you don't have the magical solutions for every problem, it can be hard not to be judgmental.

Certainly, if things aren't going that well in the parenting department, and if you've been in the position of being blamed to any extent for what may appear to an outsider as a lack of parenting skills, you know that anyone who tries to offer advice (a) doesn't know the whole story, and (b) can inadvertently (or not-so-inadvertently) imply some level of condemnation. And even if everyone else holds back advice and judgment and remains as supportive as possible to the aggrieved parents, the parents can likely to do a bang-up job of condemning themselves.

In all of my work with children and their families, it has become crystal clear to me that *when a child is having problems, and the parents are making efforts to try to help, those parents should not suffer blame.* Most are quite relieved to hear that their child's problems, and any failure of their previous efforts to deal with those problems, are not their fault.

That's right: **Any parent who cares, who is not neglectful or abusive, is not to blame for the child's problems.**

So, Who or What Can We Blame??

Without further ado, here is the reason so many parents who are making efforts to help their children surmount obstacles often do not succeed:

They have not yet found the right tools for the job.

That's right: neither the parents, nor the children, nor the teachers are the culprits. The culprits are *the methods we have at our disposal.*

They are, in a word, *upside-down.*

The last time I looked, there were over 4,000 titles on parenting at Amazon.com, and I've been told there are a total of 54,000 or so in existence. The vast majority of recommendations and approaches in those I've read are designed for the average child. Indeed, the vast majority of the approaches may have some merit for the average child; unfortunately, even most supposedly created for more intense children do little more than expand on the basic traditional dynamics for normal children. Most of the methods fall apart in one fashion or another when applied to challenging situations. And therein are great lessons to be learned for the parenting of any child.

Most methods for dealing with bad behavior in a child err in one important respect: **They shower adult energy, relationship and focus onto the child predominantly when he or she is making bad choices.** (That is why they are upside-down.)

This is a concept that may not make sense to you yet, but at some point in this first half of the book, I believe you will experience what Oprah Winfrey likes to call the "aha moment" – that moment when you grasp clearly the difference between the Nurtured Heart Approach and other approaches, particularly the way this model uses the child's thirst for adult energy, connection and recognition to propel positive rather than negative choices. This same "right-side-up" approach creates a sort of vacuum that literally *hijacks children into success* – and enthusiastically acknowledges their role in going there and in going further into greatness.

Blaming a concerned parent who is trying to fix a child's problems with an upside-down approach is like asking a carpenter to hammer in a nail with a cucumber…and blaming the carpenter when he ends up with a soggy mess and an un-hammered nail. **It's just not the right tool for the job.**

Were the parents really dysfunctional? Were they really ever the culprits? Were they really the people worthy of condemnation? I don't think so. Was the child really dysfunctional? Was he really the culprit? Did his intensity and life force merit diagnosis or medication if, within a month of experiencing the "right side up" Nurtured Heart Approach, that same child's intensity became a gift? Again: I don't think so.

I've worked with countless parents who have long struggled to find a way out of the chaos that parenting challenges can create. They think they've tried everything. But then, **when they use the Nurtured Heart Approach to reliably and predictably turn their intense child around,** *these same parents almost instantly become extraordinary.*

What better evidence is there that the techniques, not the parents, are to blame for the problems? Once these parents recognize that every other approach they've tried is *upside-down* in crucial ways, and they gain the use of a method made specifically for the job at hand, that same parent who struggled with these traditional approaches shines like the stars.

Traditional Approaches Offer Right Relationship...
at the Wrong Time

Here's an illustration of "upside-down" discipline – an example I often use in my workshops and trainings.

I was presenting an in-service program to teachers at an elementary school and arrived a half-hour before the school day ended to set up my equipment. My presentation was in the library, and nearby happened to be several large round tables where children were working independently on projects. Two teacher-librarians were stationed at the front at their console, supervising the group. For the first 15 minutes, I saw no interaction between the teachers and the children. Everyone seemed to be focused on their own tasks. Then a minor disruption occurred at one of the tables. One teacher made her way over to the child who had caused the disruption. In a caring and loving way, she put her arm around him and very kindly urged him to stay focused and not bother the other children.

Although the teacher was obviously urging the child to make better choices, and was doing so in a caring, loving way, she was inadvertently rewarding him for having made the wrong choice. The implied message to the child was, "If you disrupt the class, you get caring, loving attention and relationship, and when you don't disrupt, you are relatively invisible." **She energetically handed him a $100 bill – while telling him to stop the behavior that had earned it.**

What do you think happened next? Do you think this forestalled more disruptions?

Within minutes, the child was acting out again, this time accompanied by several others. These children got the message loud and clear that this was the way to get the adult "toy" – in this case, the teacher – to give them the connection, energy and relationship they craved.

I am in no way suggesting that this teacher stop being loving or caring, or that she resort to harsh words, lectures or reprimands to make misbehavior less energetically inviting. The truth is that even harsh words, highly imbued with energy, reward the child with relationship he or she does not tend to get when being "good" – just more $100 bills at the wrong moment in time.

If this teacher had given the child recognition in her caring, loving manner *when rules were not being broken,* the child – and his classmates – would have received a very different message.

Celebrating Problems?

If you were one of the millions who used to tune in to *The Cosby Show,* you'll recall that Dr. and Mrs. Huxtable are enlightened parents whose approach to problems involving their children consisted mostly of lectures and admonishments, which generally were laced with humor and worked like a charm in 30 minutes or less. In actuality, these fictitious parents were energetically handing out $100 bills for their children's negative choices. These same words of wisdom and reprimands, with a real-life challenging child, would only deepen that child's impression that she gets *more adventure and relationship* by way of negative actions.

Let's say Billy has been bothering his sister. His mother might pull Billy aside and say something like this: "Now, Billy, you know you're not supposed to be bothering your sister. It hurts her feelings. I think that you need to go to your room for a while and think about this, and no playing until you can apologize to her and not bother her any more." Quite the mini-lecture…even the delivery of a consequence and the use of "I-messages." All good, right?

Not from the standpoint of the Nurtured Heart Approach. What Billy's mother is really doing is accidentally giving him energy, connection, relationship and intimacy *in response to his poor choice.* And this will probably not lead him to make fewer such choices.

Most of the more commonly used approaches to parenting and discipline essentially celebrate problems and ignore (or at least downplay) the majority of successes. The Nurtured Heart Approach turns this upside-down situation right-side-up. This is the core of what makes it different from every other parenting or disciplinary approach.

Parents who become most energized and motivated toward their child *when things go wrong* are unknowingly rewarding problems. Isn't that when we typically get so inspired to teach the important lessons in our hearts and when we feel the urgency to share our words of wisdom? Unwittingly we are wheeling in the wheelbarrows of $100 bills at the very wrong moments in time.

It's not just attention. It's the much more textured weave of relationship, emotion, intimacy, caring and connection, all carrying various charges and exchanges of energy. My work has largely involved tracking the river of energy that flows underneath our words of wisdom, and I contend that our children realize and are drawn to the absolute truth of where the juice is.

The Nurtured Heart Approach is a loud and consistent refusal to inadvertently encourage children to keep on being challenging or disobedient or disrespectful. Even more, this approach tells them that there is good about them – that there is, in fact, *greatness* about them!

We can prove this to our children over and over. We break the old patterns and start them on their way to building inner wealth. Inner wealth, in turn, is the quality that enables them to make great choices without warnings, lectures or other tactics designed to scare them into "being good."

More on Greatness
The value of greatness overshadows simple goodness or absence of problems. You could consider it to be the "inner wealth" version of being a billionaire.

Greatness is an entirely different mindset, where the child has an ongoing flow of first-hand experiences that demonstrate:

- her influence on the world from other people's points of view; and
- how that influence is of great value and meaning to self, to others and to the world.

The child becomes attuned to how wonderful it is to participate in the world in a great way, and how gratifying it is to hone one's own qualities of greatness. This mindset of greatness gives breath to the child's passion for life and passion to fulfill her dreams and vision. It fills her heart with inspiration.

A child who comes to experience a core sense of greatness has a default setting on optimism. Pessimism feels wrong on her, like clothes that don't fit. She tosses them aside and eagerly, energetically sets out to find the outfit that fits just right and lets her move and stretch comfortably. Similarly, she chooses to be optimistic rather than pessimistic.

The mindset of greatness also gives the child precious clarity as to who she really is, that she matters and makes a difference – and clarity as to the confidence she feels in making choices of small and large scope. Self-doubt, fear and worry don't stand a chance of undermining this kind of clarity and resolve. Problems become just problems, not impediments.

With the Right Tools, You Can Ensure That No Child of Yours Gets Left Behind

I have seen the proof thousands of times: parents and teachers are able to help children thrive *once they have the right tools at their disposal.* That "world of difference" didn't just happen: it was the parents and teachers who were making that difference. No matter how well I do my part of teaching parents what I know to foster success, it is ultimately the parents who have taken the ball and run with it. **They essentially become the child's therapist – the agent of change – and when the tools fit the job, these "therapists" become remarkably effective and skilled.** The parents did not have to rely on counselors, teachers, therapists or pharmaceuticals to vastly improve the lives of their children; the teachers and counselors did not have to take hardline approaches to help students who seemed determined to wreck the learning environment for everyone. These changes happened as a result of the parent's or teacher's efforts to transform their approach.

Teachers and parents make the best therapists for a reason. They not only have the biggest slice of time with the child but also so much more opportunity for relationship, context and meaning within that slice of time.

A Whole-Child Approach

As a therapist, I've had several dozen children brought to me over the years because of enuresis (bedwetting). Night after night, the child rouses a parent, dripping wet and needing her odorous sheets changed; the parent, deep in sleep, is far from eager to launch the effort needed to mobilize a solution. Understandably, this issue tremendously disturbs most families.

When a family facing these circumstances seeks professional help, they are looking for a targeted "solution" – tricks or methods that will finally work to rout out this troublesome problem. Most of the families already have made many attempts to reduce the symptom; some had been advised by their pediatrician to try medications or simple, common-sense remedies like restricting water intake in the evenings. Others had tried devices like plastic sheets with alarms that go off when moisture is detected. Although these remedies do work for some, they did not work for the families that came to me for help.

These parents expected their visit with me to yield one more round of "let's try this next"…some reward system involving complicated charts and stickers, perhaps, or some consequence involving the child cleaning up. They were expecting yet another intervention – perhaps more brilliant or more clever, but still directly linked to the symptom – hopefully, the one that would finally make the problem disappear.

The family was usually surprised when I informed them that I could, indeed, help them with this problem…but that we weren't going to focus on the symptom of enuresis specifically. I would then explain that a deeper level of healing, involving the whole child, is key. I would tell them: "I can help you with this problem. It consistently heals in a matter of a month or so, often faster."

I'd see their faces brighten, but their expressions often gave way to one of confusion as I told them: *It's crucial that we not work directly with the symptom at all. I can teach you an alternate approach to parenting your child…an alternate philosophy of how children best respond and come to feel successful. If all goes well, within a few weeks you will witness a deep transformation in the way your child feels about life, about who he is, and about his experience of feeling successful. As that takes place, your child will stop bedwetting on his own, with no urging or admonishments on your part.*

As the parents tried to digest this concept of a whole-child intervention, I'd go on:

As a child really feels successful about himself, at an entirely new level, and experiences his inner wealth in a new way, the last thing he wants to do is pee in the wrong places at the wrong times. He will figure out his own solution; no one will have to tell him how to do it. And in most instances, traditional approaches can't accomplish this level of inner wealth. In fact, they can easily make the situation worse. And then I would begin to tell them about the Nurtured Heart Approach.

As it turns out, this approach, suited as it is for use with every child, is not optimally used to target specific behaviors. It's not a scalpel one can use to address and excise a specific troublesome behavior. In other words: if your child has been doing one specific thing that's driving you nuts and causing disruptions, you can't single out that thing and rub it out with targeted use of this approach. This approach is for every child, and it is for the *whole child.*

Specifically targeting a single type of problem behavior keeps the focus riveted on the problem itself, still feeding it all the energy it requires to grow bigger and more persistent. That problem becomes charged when it accumulates lots of relationship and energy and concern from everyone around the child. This energy stacks the deck, so to speak, giving the child incontrovertible first-hand evidence that keeping this problem alive means plenty of connection – even a sense of intimacy with his parents. In contrast, the specific problem can serve a grander purpose – that of providing the impetus to help move the child's sense of self to a higher order entirely.

Children come to feel that they are relatively invisible when problems are not happening and become increasingly convinced that there's much more "life force" available through the response of others to adversity. If I'm a child with some such issue – and all children have issues from time to time – it's so easy for me to perceive that the issue is bigger than life itself…that the problem comprises a disproportionately large part of who I am.

When parents learn to address the *whole child,* using the approach you are learning in these pages, they find that whatever specific problems they were facing recede as their child is drawn, as if by gravity, into a realm of inner wealth and personal power. The bottom line is that the child comes to feel seen, recognized and appreciated. The child takes on a new sense of greatness because we are shining the light of greatness in her eyes when the timing is right-side up, when the child is choosing not to misbehave. We are consciously and purposefully nurturing the many aspects of the whole child.

Normal, Traditional Approaches Fall Short
Normal approaches for parenting and teaching are designed for the average child. They fail to be encompassing enough for the challenging child, essentially falling apart when things start to go wrong. And whether the child is average or challenging, these conventional approaches do not capitalize sufficiently on the opportunity to bring the child into a "portfolio of success" *when things are going well.* Ordinary strategies attempt to reinforce good choices when things are going well but they are typically both under-energized in that regard and less able to irrefutably make the child aware of the greatness inherent in those good choices.

Think about this: The words we use to describe success – whether with our children or with others – are skimpy in comparison to the vivid language we employ to describe failure. When things are going wrong, it is so easy to see and elaborate upon the minutest details. It is so easy, despite our intention for our children to succeed, to accidentally cram their portfolios with evidence that we are so much more excited about their shortcomings. Emphasis on their poor choices conveys to them vivid images of their lack of capacity in important areas of life.

The last thing anyone would every do is give a child $100 for breaking a rule or for otherwise falling short; energetically, we inadvertently do it all the time by way of conventional parenting recommendations: bigger responses and more relationship *when things are going wrong.*

The Nurtured Heart Approach encourages parents not to attack problems, but to give problems little or no energy aside from a quick, effective result/reset and to give all the focus, recognition and energy to successes. And successes are far more abundant than you might think at this juncture. You'll soon see that successes are enormously abundant in the life of even the most "challenging" child…and that you can recognize your children's successes in a vivid, energized manner that eclipses traditional ways of offering recognition by a country mile.

This kind of recognition is the foundation of the Nurtured Heart Approach. It is the right tool for building within your children something I call *inner wealth*. This inner wealth is the foundation upon which the flourishing child develops – and, possibly, the foundation upon which the future of civilization may rely.

The Big Picture: Our Children's Inner Wealth May Decide the Future

Humans love drama. We revel in the excitement of risk and conflict, of competition and difficulty. We love to talk about what's wrong. But I submit that a time has arrived in human history where we must find that new trajectory that allows us to raise our children in ways that make happiness, confidence, inner peace, cooperation and GREATNESS the exciting measure of our priorities…where these qualities hold more promise and are far more enticing than drama, conflict, competition and difficulty. This model is a path to that shift.

We may no longer have the luxury of using the more traditional approaches. They not only fail us with our challenging children – and the world is certainly seeing more challenging children – but these approaches fall short in helping conventionally successful, well-behaved children become strong enough on the inside – as strong on the inside as they can possibly be.

Doesn't the world hold bigger challenges for every child? The world is different today than it was even a decade ago. The events of September 11, 2001, and the conflicts that have followed have altered the American psyche, and although our children may not quite grasp the impact of those events and conflicts, the changing attitudes, pressures and anxieties of adults around them have certainly altered their worlds, too. And then there's global warming – another problem we're likely to leave to today's children to solve, at least in part.

The Power of Media and Materialism

Today's pressures and difficulties are exacerbated by ever more pervasive media. In the 1970s, young people "tuned in, turned on and dropped out" with drugs, free love and civil disobedience; now, they do it with the Web, music piped directly into their ears from digital music players, cell phones and video games (and, in some cases, sex and drugs). Material pleasures are easily accessible to almost every child, and they often make up a huge part of our young people's identities and focus. And it's so much easier to plug in and tune out with all this fantastic entertainment than ever before.

Entertainment and media can be wonderful for children who have abundant inner wealth, but those who don't can end up sucked in by the marketing machine, feeling as though they are incomplete and inadequate without the latest, hottest outfit, gadget or other costly item.

Today, children have unprecedented exposure to depictions of material wealth and luxury in the media. Lacking strong inner wealth and direction, that's what they end up wanting and longing for. Its allure is powerful.

"Fame Junkies" and the Changing American Dream

Jake Halpern, a National Public Radio commentator and the author of *Fame Junkies: The Truth Behind America's Favorite Addiction,* commissioned a study of 653 teens in Rochester, New York. He found that kids idolized celebrities – including musicians, sports heroes and movie stars – far more than any other heroes. No surprise to any parent reading these words, right? Kids don't know the names of political leaders or what's going on in the world, but they do know what's happening in the life of Brad Pitt or Britney Spears.

Nearly 44 percent of the teenage girls Halpern interviewed said that they would rather be a celebrity's personal assistant than a CEO, a U.S. senator, the president of Yale or Harvard or a Navy SEAL when they grew up. Thirty-one percent of the boys and girls surveyed said they wanted to be famous celebrities. When offered the options of becoming stronger, smarter, famous or beautiful, about half of the boys said they'd rather be famous than more intelligent, and more girls chose fame over greater intelligence as well.

Kids also widely dream of being millionaires. The allure of big money and luxurious trappings make celebrity and big-money professions seem like the path of least resistance to many kids – despite the fact that there are only about 2.7 million millionaires in the U.S., a nation of about 300 million people.

I believe that true power is derived from wisdom emanating from the depths of the heart, body, mind and soul. When the right tools are applied by a parent, he or she shows the child what it is to be a powerful hero…that it isn't about being prettier than everyone else, or about having more money or more celebrity, but rather about the wisdom and other qualities of greatness we bring forth through our thoughts, words and actions. Parenting in a way that helps a child manifest her greatness is something I consider to be an act of heroism. And in developing greatness, the child emerges as a powerful hero as well. In all my years of working with this approach, I have yet to find that part fail to unfold.

Instead of letting our children get sucked into chasing the carrot of wealth or celebrity, we can make a shift that will enable every child to succeed in an inherently unfair and unequal socioeconomic system. We can bring out their inner wealth so powerfully that they *want* to live in coexistence and cooperation rather than in violent competition. And this can be done whether your children are very young or nearly grown, as long as you use the appropriate transformative tools. That won't preclude them being a millionaire or a star, but if so they will live that life in a more intelligent, compassionate, enjoyable and balanced way.

Just as children who are stuck using their intensities in negative ways can move exponentially further down that path, children who are helped to thrive and abide in the vast realm of success can grow exponentially in that direction. Success can become their place of residence – their compass and guiding force. Children who become the heir to the real fortune, inner wealth, are guaranteed the much greater fate of living their dreams and purpose, being clear about what they truly want and need, and having the determination and clarity to steer clear of relationships and paths that waste their time or interfere with their higher path of greatness.

And the first step, for you, is to grasp a concept you've read about here already: *inner wealth.*

CHAPTER THREE

Beyond Self-Esteem: Instilling Inner Wealth

If there is radiance in the soul, it will abound in the family. If there is radiance in the family, it will be abundant in the community. If there is radiance in the community, it will grow in the nation. If there is radiance in the nation, the universe will flourish.
– Lao Tsu

This happens every day: A child winds up in the court system, having been inveigled by others to break the law. A good child gets in trouble. Would the child have done it if she were stronger on the inside? If only she had the strength to say no when she knew she was being urged to do something she knew was wrong!

Every parent is faced with the challenge of trying to strengthen their children enough so they will stay out of trouble. Most do so by verbally urging them to be stronger...to think better....to use better judgment. But how is this inner strength really achieved?

The ultimate goal of this book is to give you tools that can be used to transform who your children think they are, the life they think they will have. These tools will enable you to give them abundant evidence that they are valuable, good, competent and able to cope well with life. In the lexicon of the Nurtured Heart Approach, we say that the goal of the approach is to create *inner wealth*.

Inner wealth is the thing that enables human beings to cope, be happy, and grow within ourselves and with other people. It is multi-faceted. It is deeply connected to our feeling that we are part of humanity, significantly and meaningfully, just by virtue of being alive. It is deeply connected to our ability to fearlessly be in the NOW. Inner wealth is what we strive to instill in our children with this approach.

You might think of inner wealth as "self-confidence" or "self-esteem" or perhaps "believing in yourself." You would be right if you made these connections, but you wouldn't have the full picture.

Self-Esteem and Inner Wealth

One friend of mine, who happens to be a teacher, sees the intensity and acting-out of so many children not as a curse but a blessing. "They're *demanding* something that they really need from teachers," she told me. "They don't have any idea how to talk about this thing they need, but they know they need something, and they need it badly."

From what I've seen in classrooms and homes where the Nurtured Heart Approach is implemented, I think I know what it is these children need – actually *crave*, in a deep way. It's inner wealth. They need to have the light of their greatness shone upon them. Once this happens, this profound hunger abates. You can see them clicking into their own greatness. You can see them relaxing into it. And self-esteem, as lovely as it might be, doesn't go far enough into that greatness to fill the void.

Certainly, self-confidence and self-esteem are essential for a happy, fulfilling life. Many wise people have spoken out about this sometimes elusive quality. Eleanor Roosevelt famously said, "No one can make you feel inferior without your permission." Here are some of the Dalai Lama's thoughts on the topic of self-confidence:

> Human potential is the same for all. Your feeling, "I am of no value," is wrong. Absolutely wrong...With the realization of one's own potential and self-confidence in one's ability, one can build a better world. According to my own experience, self-confidence is very important. That sort of confidence is not a blind one; it is an awareness of one's own potential. On that basis, human beings can transform themselves by increasing the good qualities and reducing the negative qualities.

And here are some well-known words from Marianne Williamson in *A Return to Love:*

> Our deepest fear is not that we are inadequate. Our deepest fear is that we are powerful beyond measure.

It is our light, not our darkness, that most frightens us. We ask ourselves, Who am I to be brilliant, gorgeous, talented, fabulous?

Actually, who are you not to be? You are a child of God. Your playing small does not serve the world. There is nothing enlightened about shrinking so that other people won't feel insecure around you. We are all meant to shine, as children do. We were born to make manifest the glory of God that is within us. It's not just in some of us; it's in everyone. And as we let our own light shine, we unconsciously give other people permission to do the same. As we are liberated from our own fear, our presence automatically liberates others.

In the last few decades of the 20th century, the "self-esteem movement" exhorted every person to build their self-esteem to solve virtually any problem they were facing.

Interestingly, although educators and parents were told that giving children increased self-esteem would help them achieve better in school and do better in life, the research on the subject hasn't proven this to be correct. When children are told to accept, realize, approve of, and love themselves *no matter what,* they don't achieve better in school. When children are told to have self-esteem, but aren't given the day-to-day input that actually creates that esteem, the message ultimately rings hollow.

The question that didn't get answered adequately during the self-esteem revolution was: How do you *get* self-esteem if you're short on it? Can you cause it to materialize by sheer force of will? Can you impact others by sharing the thinking or theory of why it would be a good idea to have more of it? Can you create it by being good at something – perhaps baseball or chess or math? Can you be talked into it by great teachers, thinkers or politicians? Maybe, but these methods don't seem to be reliable enough to cover the job of building this quality in every child.

I maintain that a crucial element is missing in this widely accepted concept of self-esteem. It lacks the depth and honesty that comes from *actual, frequent experiences of being held in esteem...*of being appreciated not only for doing things right and for doing the right things but for doing the right things with a quality of greatness.

When we try to imbue self-esteem without those actual experiences of appreciation and gratitude – by using parenting and disciplinary techniques that accidentally celebrate the child for making wrong choices – it's like slipping the child that $100 bill for bad behavior, then telling the child, "Hey, you can do it, you *can* feel great about yourself!" Parents and teachers wind up working at cross-purposes.

Imagine yourself at work, making a big blunder, then having someone pay you extra money and tell you how fabulous you are. This would be confusing enough for an adult; imagine how confusing it is for a child.

The Spiritual Realm

> *...I think of each life as a flower, as common as a field daisy,*
> *and as singular...*
> – Mary Oliver

Inner wealth may best be described as a spiritual endeavor, so no definition strictly from psychology can do it justice. As you'll see, inner wealth takes the self-esteem concept up a few notches, from a shallow psychological catch-phrase to a spiritual odyssey – a journey into who each person really is in the fullest sense.

If you are a person of faith, you may think of inner wealth in terms of being full of Holy Spirit or of being a manifestation of God's energy and will on Earth. But that doesn't quite cover it, either.

Religious traditions throughout history have voiced ideas that parallel this concept of inner wealth. Buddhism teaches that every sentient being has the capacity to become enlightened and fully perfected. Sufis feel that it is through us that God discovers himself and evolves to greater manifestation of divine qualities. The Hindu faith of Vedanta celebrates each person as already perfect. Christian doctrine calls upon us to love our neighbors as ourselves and equates love of God with love of self; we are made in God's image and so should love ourselves as we love Him. Jesus manifested greatness in his life-time. He felt that the purpose of his life was to bear witness to the truth, and he had the inner wealth to do so. Perhaps that truth is the path of greatness itself. Maybe that path was easier for him because people clearly attributed greatness to him from birth.

Wouldn't it be interesting if all God's children were clearly attributed with greatness from birth? What might that look like?

All of these concepts and ideas are relevant to inner wealth. What does it take to go beyond just coping, to achieve greatness, to be truly happy in our spirits and to thrive? The Nurtured Heart Approach gives you the tools to build self-esteem *and* inner wealth, systematically. It does so by relentlessly *creating experiences of success and greatness,* one after the other, shining the light of those many qualities that comprise greatness in the eyes of our children.

The accumulation of these personal first-hand experiences of feeling appreciated and recognized and of feeling a sense of greatness becomes integral to one's inner sense of self. It's a much sweeter way to live one's life. This sense of manifesting one's gifts of greatness becomes like the current of a river, living in a continuous, flowing, pervasive presence of knowing of "I can" and "I am." In the face of this, self-doubt and worry evaporate.

Inner Wealth Helps Us Remain in the Present Moment

Wherever you go, there you are.
– Jon Kabat-Zinn, M.D.

With inner wealth, one can have more of the resolve and strength required to *stay in the moment*. Rather than jumping away from pain, anger or fear like a cat off a hot tin roof, inner wealth gives the comfort and strength required to make a measured and wise choice about where to go next, even when uncomfortable about the current situation. With inner wealth, each moment is a fresh new moment; you can die to every past moment, allowing for what Zen calls "beginner's mind" – an infant's view of the wondrous world. There is a release of preconceptions and a huge openness to learning and fresh experience. Each new moment is brimming with information about what is called for; cultivating inner wealth in our children allows them to truly listen.

A child shifted into the realm of inner wealth has great adaptability and flexibility. There is less fear of the unknown. Rather than seeking a world that seems safe because it is black and white and inflexible, with strict codes of morality and behavior imposed from outside, the child with inner wealth can tolerate the ambiguity of a world that is always evolving and changing. It is this child who is always prepared to make "right choices" from the inside out.

Most adults carry stagnant points of view from the past and complex fears and hopes about the future. For adults, the path back to the now is rewarding, but not easy. Practices like meditation, yoga, religious observance, the arts, or studying the works of spiritual teachers can all help. Practicing the Nurtured Heart Approach will also help to center you squarely in the present moment.

Children are so much closer to that perfect state of presence into which we are all born. Being in the moment is second nature for them – until life teaches them otherwise. As you learn to apply the Nurtured Heart Approach with your children, you will be giving them the amazing gift of learning to live in the present moment as they gain important tools for moving into their futures.

Inner wealth is a growing and deepening sense of:
Spirit

Knowing

Optimism

Being lovable

Having much to give

Being filled with life force – and not being afraid of it

Being open to, less afraid of, and non-resistant to change

Being excited about the prospects of life and of living life fully

Being able to handle strong feelings

Being unafraid of intimacy

Being less likely to be consumed by anxiety, stress and depression

Cultivating the ability to default to success

Being better connected to one's body – and taking better care of it as a result

Wonder and awe

Trust and faith

Greatness, meaning and purpose

Enjoyment and fulfillment

Holding great intentions

Loving life, self and others

Seeing what is true and wanting to live in truthfulness

Having ready access to the "inner compass" that best guides intuition – that wise whisper into one's ear

Being present to self and others, in the moment

Being in true power of body, heart and soul collab-oratively

Being willing to give away power – because it doesn't deplete one's supply

Having the courage to create, express and adapt to whatever is next

Happiness in everyday life – no need for thrill-seeking

Caring deeply for all life on the planet

Seeing beauty: of nature, art, the universe, life itself

Moving away from addictive patterns

Taking responsibility for one's contributions to the world – by way of one's choices

Making the world a softer place by giving support and kindness to others

Seeing the beauty of grace in the world

Being thankful, appreciative, grateful and forgiving

Being principled and making honorable decisions

Using excellent judgment and making intelligent decisions

Being respectful

Being reverent

Being willing to enjoy the journey into the unknown – into the mystery

Living in one's heart

Being inspired to greatness

Believing in one's greatness

Inner wealth supports one's ability to *default to success,* which changes many of the little (and big) annoyances of life into opportunities. Rather than fearing the worst, one looks for the bright side. As success is created and manifested, more of the same is attracted. A child who possesses a core sense of inner wealth cannot sustain pessimism. A child with inner wealth resets quickly from a problem mode to the next new moment of positivity.

Children with inner wealth want a good night's sleep; they want to be at school on time; they want to eat well. They don't resist good self-care, and they often don't even have to be told how to take good care of their bodies; they figure it out for themselves.

The child with inner wealth is much more likely to connect with his "source" in a core way, embracing a spirituality of his own making. He will know how to find his connection to Spirit – whether that is God or nature or some other source – and know to go there when he perceives signs of disconnection.

Those who experience an inner life of scarcity replicate scarcity wherever they go. Conversely, inner wealth brings a feeling of connection and abundance – an inner experience of prosperity that creates a desire to give to others, without depleting one's self. If a child comes to trust her inner strength and guidance, she can throw herself into life that much more fully. She can freely expend life force, because she comes to trust that, in fully expending that life force, it is replenished that much more fully – like exhaling all the breath out of the body, really wringing it out, and allowing for the sweet inhalation to drift back in effortlessly.

The child with inner wealth is not going to conform for the sake of conformity, or rebel for the sake of rebellion. Those with inner wealth experience a remarkable facility for good judgment, forgiveness and appreciation. Parents of children with inner wealth will find themselves surprisingly trusting of their child's judgment and wisdom, even during the teen years.

One of the beautiful aspects of this approach is that your own concept of inner wealth will continually expand and change. There is always much to recognize and celebrate. Something is always going well, even when the big picture starts out looking bleak.

Take just a few factors listed above and start to observe them in yourself and others. As you progress along in developing your child's inner wealth, you can also experiment with building your own inner wealth by opportunistically noting and enjoying *your* efforts and successes. Experiment with new and expanded "inner wealth vocabulary." Think about variations on the themes of appreciation and recognition. In the clutter and chatter of the day, find a way to awaken your heart to greatness – especially when you are feeling overwhelmed. Make it your mission to infuse your heart with these messages.

Building Inner Wealth

When mindfulness embraces those we love, they bloom like flowers.
– Thich Nhat Hanh

Inner wealth enables children to use good judgment, make good choices, resist exploitation, choose good partners and friends, think of the future while being attuned to the needs of the moment, cope with adversity, take risks, and find courage and love. When a child resides in the realm of inner wealth, he has the equivalent of a GPS guidance system. That guidance system represents the hand that's always present, gently tweaking the direction of his life in a positive route.

The strength and wisdom that result from inner wealth helps children feel comfortable in being amazing; in experiencing the amazing NOW as opposed to fear-based living in the past or the future; and amazement and wonder in living life and manifesting their purpose and dreams. It helps them really drink the sweetness of life and bring joy to others.

To build inner wealth is to find a myriad number of ways to recognize, convey and celebrate a child's heart, spirit and character. We fearlessly, relentlessly pursue evidence with which to validate qualities of greatness.

Building inner wealth in our children requires that:

- We find this evidence (of qualities of inner wealth) in what they do; in what they *don't* do; and in their intentions, hopes and successes...and even their failures.
- We do not inadvertently energize poor choices by giving relationship and energy in response to those choices.
- We strive to have a laser-like focus on any steps the child takes toward success.
- We remain strict. There is always a consequence for any rule broken – along with a loving and simple way to move on to the next NOW of success, which amounts to a built-in way of freely offering forgiveness.

- We give consequences for poor choices, *even while having complete faith in the child's ability to do better* – and quickly finding reason to justify that faith.

Beginning to Explore New Reflections: Beyond "Thank You" and "Good Job"

Let's say you tell your child, "We have a few extra things to do tonight after dinner so we need to eat early. I'd like you to turn off the TV and go wash up and come right away to the dinner table." Let's assume the child follows the request right away in a cooperative manner, and let's further assume that you, the parent, are generally a positive person, so you make a point of saying something appreciative to your child. What are some of the most common positive acknowledgments?

When I ask this question in seminars, mostly consisting of therapists and educators who generally have a far more expansive repertoire of positive responses than the general public, the most frequently called out answers are "thank you," "good job," "very good," "I appreciate that," "way to go" and "excellent." At this point in the seminar setting, I typically proceed with a little experiment in the room. I look out into the audience, directly eying several people, and dole out these same simple appreciations. Then I say, "Obviously, I am pleased with something. Can anyone whom I just spoke to, or any of the other intelligent people in this room, tell me specifically what I'm so pleased about?"

The people in the room always look completely stumped – and they see, in a flash, how vague these general statements and praises really are. They transmit very little information to the person on the receiving end. I go on: "If this group of intelligent adults doesn't know what I'm referring to when I say 'good job,' then what are the chances that our children really know?"

Even when I observe the classrooms of teachers who have been described as "highly positive," I consistently hear the vague and general statements of "good job" and "thank you" sprinkled with a few more specific statements of appreciation such as "thanks for being focused," "thanks for staying seated" and "thank you for being quiet."

Would you want these kinds of tributes printed in your obituary or your epitaph? *She was quiet in school. He sat in his chair until dismissed.*

This is no tribute to your brilliant life or your great attributes as a contributing human being on this planet! It's a way of "being positive" that's designed not to foster each child's special qualities of greatness, but to keep everyone in line so that basic standards can be met.

On more than one occasion, in such a so-called "positive" classroom, I've had an almost uncontrollable urge to shout: "There is so much more to who we are as human beings than being able to sit still and be quiet!" Every one of these children has admirable and important qualities and skills that need to be seen, acknowledged and cultivated!

Some of these teachers seemed to be using statements from that old list of '100 Ways to Praise a Child.' That list is made up of variations of the same old worn statements. They lack the specificity and energy that inner wealth-building requires.

When we say "thank you" or "good job," how much energy are we radiating? Is it Tigger, bounding and bouncing and fun, or Eeyore, sad and slow? Or somewhere in between? Typically, when I ask about this in seminars, the consensus is that the energy radiated when we make statements of ordinary praise is at the modest end of the continuum.

Let's examine a second scenario. This time you say the very same thing to your child (about needing to get things done after dinner and instructing the child to turn off the TV, wash up, come to the table). Your child responds by saying, "Okay, but can I just watch another minute?" You happen to be in a very good mood this day and say, "All right. One more minute." A few minutes later, you come back, your mood just barely beginning to lose its luster, and your child begs, "Please, just another minute, it's the best part of the show!" Again, feeling great about the day and life in general, you stay relaxed and calm and easily give in to another few minutes.

How many rounds of this are you up for? Can you see that checking up on the child and having words with him around his refusal to comply with your request is a more highly energized response than even the usual "good job" or "excellent"? The child can easily discern that a lot more energy, time, words, relationship and (probably) animation transpire in relation to lack of cooperation.

Does a child need to put a blood pressure cuff around your arm to notice that you're getting more and more energized under these circumstances? Can a child discern when there's more in general? Sure! Can't we all? If I hold up a five and a 50 and ask which one you want, how many of you will choose the five? How long did that take you to figure out? We have this immediate knowing of how much more we can acquire with 50. I don't even have to say five or 50 of what! And children are particularly talented in this regard, as any parent knows who's had to settle endless squabbles over which child got more dessert or a longer turn with a valued toy.

The positive remarks we often make to our children are limited reflections of the extent to which the child is valued. This is not to say that parents do not profoundly love and value their children. But "good job" and "thank you" type praises pale in comparison to statements crafted as much more precise, interesting reflections of the truth of a child's impact on this planet. We can do better. We can show them in incontestable terms that they are great – we can shine their own light back onto them in a much more vivid way than "thank you" and "good job" allow.

Let's say you're in the toy store with your child, who has just asked you for a toy. You say "no" and that it's time to leave. The child sighs sadly and turns to head for the door. You stop him outside, get down to his level, look in his eyes and say: *I appreciate the choice you just made. You somehow decided not to argue. I feel that didn't just happen. You used good judgment and inner wisdom and made the big effort needed to walk away, even though you were unhappy when I told you that you couldn't have that toy. Thank you for making that successful choice.*

A statement like this reflects back to the child an infinitely more powerful and encompassing level of success, giving his eyes and ears a first-hand experience of his positive impact on another. *Because it is woven into a real-life experience, it is irrefutable – can't be defended against – in contrast to general and global statements of praise that can easily hit the radar as just more of the same and be taken down by the child's defenses.* Because it feels irrefutable, it is almost like an immediate download of new software that gives the child the feeling "this is who I really am." It's not a question of whether I can or can't: I *am* someone with these qualities. This is the part that I have found to be so powerful in my work with children.

First-Hand Experiences

If I want to learn something new like tennis or yoga, do I do so by sitting in a chair, watching a video of someone else doing it? Watching a video might provide me with important learning points. But alone, that experience will not allow me to integrate what I see into my muscles, bones and sinews. It's a second-hand experience until I immerse myself in the activity. Then I can realize not only the direct benefits of the activity, but the psychological benefit of realizing that there is no longer a question of whether I can or can't do this activity. I *am* doing it. And my inner wealth is growing – and it'll do so even more if a trusted adult reflects it all back to me with love and excitement.

This is another way of talking about "being in the now" or being in the moment: You and your child are together in this very moment, where you're giving him access to your experience of his being successful – in a manner that creates a first-hand experience for him; you both get to share in and enjoy that experience together.

How often do you shower your child with earnest words of wisdom that pour from the fountain of your own hard-earned life experience? Next time you find yourself doing this, notice how your persuasive language most frequently falls into the realm of straightforward, rational and reasonable dialogue – especially when perceived poor choices have been made. Somehow, parents have come to think that if they could just choose exactly the right words to convey their unimpeachable logic to the child, they can convince her to make better choices in the future. We act as if it is a straightforward and linear process – often conveniently forgetting how we tuned out our own parents' lectures when we were children.

Any lecture, eloquent though it may be, provides the child with powerful first-hand evidence of failure. *Here you are, being celebrated energetically for your lack of responsibility, for your inability to control your temper, for your inconsiderateness of someone else's feelings, for breaking the rules. Again.*

In contrast, we need to celebrate important qualities *when the adversity is not happening.* The infusion of adult energy in those moments gives the child an experience of success instead of a lecture that points out all the ways in which he falls short. This is where inner wealth starts and expands.

In the Nurtured Heart Approach, we employ strategies that actively honor and reflect, in a truthful and deep manner, that our children are celebrated for their decisions, judgments and wisdom. But we go beyond that, letting them know they embody the positive qualities that reflect greatness. It's not a question of whether they can embody a particular quality in the future, or whether they did so in the past. We tell them, "You *are* embodying this quality. Here you are now, doing so, successfully." That's a *first-hand experience of success.*

Your Energy and Focus Trump Your Words

Whether meaning to or not, parents are always sending messages to their children about what they value. You may think you're sending a specific, carefully composed message with your words when you give a long-winded lecture, but your energetic messages shout far more loudly to your children. If the energy doesn't jive with the words, the communication has much less chance of being clearly received or incorporated as intended into the child's awareness and behaviors.

Children are exquisitely sensitive to energetic messages. At the same time, they are usually closed to verbal messages that arrive at moments of adversity. They are far less moved or influenced by verbal descriptions of theories and notions ("You should not blah, blah, you really should blah, blah, it's just not RIGHT, don't you want to be GOOD?") than they are by the appropriate application of energy given to the good choices and withdrawn from the bad.

Computer experts will tell you that there's more to what appears on the screen than meets the eye: there's an underlying level, a language or code, that runs underneath the surface, and it's that unseen reality that actually runs the show. I'm certain that the very same is true in relation to our children.

Children are also responding to an underlying level that runs beneath the surface. The Nurtured Heart Approach's techniques take advantage of this. In this approach, the communication happens at the heart level, that underlying energetic realm where truth rings through so clearly. It cuts right through the blockades created by the mind and the body, and this is why it works so well and so easily.

If children who are used to upside-down approaches end up wired wrong, we have to change the wiring to get the juice to the right places at the right times – to get through those mental and physical blocks they have already established in the course of their short stays on Earth. We use specific techniques (described in full in the second half of this book) to get to the fuse box and rearrange the crossed wires – allowing our messages to reach their intended purpose and have their effect, without all the screaming, lecturing and conflict many of us have become accustomed to.

Why Pep Talks Don't Work

Inner wealth cannot be cultivated with pep talks, which are generally given to encourage specific desired qualities: "I *know* you can make your own bed…you *can* be responsible… come on, let's see you do it!"

These backfire because, despite your energized cheerleading, the underlying message is still, "I see you have not done what you are supposed to. You are falling short. You are not successful." You are still giving out the energy-laden $100 bills at the wrong moments.

Instead, if we want to reinforce the desirable quality of responsibility, we find moments where the child *is* being responsible. "I see you're putting your dirty clothes in the hamper. That really shows responsibility, and I so appreciate the help keeping the house neat and tidy." And if we want to zoom it to the next level of greatness, we can add: "Being responsible and cooperative are qualities of greatness. I appreciate that you are being great in these ways."

And we are then just rekindling the fire of that quality – reloading the update of that software of greatness.

Where pep talks and lectures attempt to encourage specific desired qualities or actions, typically delivered when things aren't going well (upside-down), the Nurtured Heart Approach weaves the very same qualities and actions into the fabric of the child's actual experience through a positive construction of the moment. The parent verbally cherishes those qualities as they occur in real time, helping the child see that he is already in possession of that quality – that today, right now, he embodies it. It's not something he has to strive for; it's already inside him.

CHAPTER FOUR

Shamu's Secret, the Toll-taker's Dance, and the Overarching Intention of Choosing to See and Create Greatness

Cultivating inner wealth in your child requires that you learn to see and colorfully acknowledge his successes. And successes, as you'll see from the following three analogies that form the foundation of this approach, are far easier to find than you might think. All three of these concepts contribute to the overarching intention of *choosing to see greatness* and *creating greatness*.

Shamu's Leap

Most people know that Shamu is a performing orca whale. Not everyone realizes, however, that many such whales perform in theme parks all over the world under the same famous name. Although whales do jump in the wild, they don't jump anywhere near the heights typically achieved once these intelligent sea mammals are trained to perform. Have you ever considered how trainers might persuade these nearly 10-ton whales to jump over a rope 22 feet above the surface of the water?

This was the trick Shamu needed to learn in order to draw the big crowds week after week: to leap over that rope any time his trainers gave the signal. It wouldn't be much fun for the audiences if Shamu jumped an hour after he got the signal, or on the other side of the tank, away from the rope.

His trainers knew an approach to accomplishing their goals that would get Shamu to jump that rope on command, eliciting *oooohs* and *ahhhhhs* from one delighted audience after another. The trainers had the *right tools for this job*, which they had derived from their own education and experience.

They knew that you can't start the training by hanging a bucket of fish 22 feet in the air, or by merely commanding Shamu to jump and expecting him to do so. In the beginning, Shamu didn't even know his name or what a rope was, so the chances of obtaining success this way were zero. The proper connections had not yet been linked up with Shamu's natural talents.

Most people, when asked to try to figure out how this was done, guess that the rope started out lower, but very few people figure out that the rope was actually *under the water*, at the very bottom of the tank.

Shamu was appreciated, patted, loved and rewarded whenever he happened to cruise over the rope in his travels around the tank. This intelligent animal made the connection fairly quickly that the good stuff came when he went over the twisted thing we humans call a rope. Then the trainers could slowly and incrementally raise the rope, and he kept on leaping, willingly and happily, knowing his reward lay on the other side.

The willingness of the trainers to start with the rope at the bottom derived from their willingness to **create successes that would not otherwise exist.** This, in turn, led directly to a faster path of learning and a level of attainment well beyond what would normally occur.

You are setting out to build a very similar connection for your child. Once your child grasps the link between the *internal feeling of success* and your response in terms of the energy, relationship and emotional reaction you demonstrate, she will begin to seek and integrate success into every aspect of her life. Before long, success becomes second nature.

Shamu's Example: Catching Goodness vs. Creating Goodness
In practice, this is slightly different from the concept of *catching* the child doing good, but rather about *creating* it. *It's really about creating successes that wouldn't otherwise exist.*

If I'm the parent of a difficult child, and I try to follow the common parenting edict to "catch the child being good" and comment on it, I might end up waiting an awfully long time. We need a tool that doesn't leave us in this disadvantaged, disempowered position. It is much harder for us to discern little bits of success and goodness than to spot and comment on what is wrong. We are fluent in the language of failure, of falling short. We can glibly go on and on about what's out of order, incorrect or awry, but we tend to have a flat language of success.

If you find ways to honor and celebrate the child for good judgment, thoughtfulness and wisdom, and to cease giving energy to his poor choices, you can keep moving that figurative rope to higher and higher planes of the child's greatness.

And the best part of working with children instead of whales, aside from the fact you won't need a pail of fish or a wetsuit, is that the child will know when to help you raise the rope.

The Dance of the Toll-taker

I first heard the story of the Oakland-Bay Bridge tollbooth attendant from a college professor who drove across the Bay Bridge one morning when there was little traffic. As he approached the tollbooths, he rolled down the window and heard old rock-and-roll dance music blaring from a nearby radio.

He looked around for the source of the tunes and observed that a tollbooth attendant several lanes away was grooving to the beat and having a great time. The professor was able to drive up to the dancing attendant's lane. As he pulled up to the booth, he commented, "It looks like you're having the time of your life."

The tollbooth attendant replied, "Of course. I have the best job in the world and the best office in the world." The driver asked him what he meant.

"I get to be out here listening to my favorite tunes, doing my own thing and meeting nice people," the attendant told him. "What executive do you know who has an office with four glass walls and a view that comes even close to this one? I can look west and just about see the ocean. I can look north and south and see beautiful views of the bay, and I can look east and see the mainland. If I work the early shift, I can see the sunrise. And if I work later, I can see the sunset. With all these clouds, the view is different every day. Nothing can compare to this. Besides, I'm going to be a dancer, and I'm getting paid to practice!"

The professor gestured to the other tollbooths: "What about the other attendants? They don't seem to be having the time of their lives."

The response was, "Oh, those guys in the stand-up coffins! They're no fun."

Toll-taker's Lesson: Choosing the Way We See Things
You've known for a long time that everything is subject to how we choose to view it. But it's so easy to forget, in the grind of daily life, that we hold that option card. Is the cup half-full or half-empty? It's our call.

Imagine yourself in both situations: in that tollbooth, music blaring, with the incredible attitude of the tollbooth attendant; or in that same tollbooth, with the "stand-up coffin" mindset, dreading another day of annoying pollution, noise, traffic and headaches.

It's not unlike clicking a shutter of a camera and capturing the truth of the frame that is NOW. We get to construe that moment and attribute meaning, value and greatness in any way we wish.

It's not only our choice: **we get to choose at any given moment.**

The less enthralled toll-takers could show up at work in a funk and then choose to see things differently at any given moment of their shift. Similarly, parents can choose to view the everyday events that comprise their lives and their children's lives in a positive, "glass-half-full" manner. This will enable you to see successes, victories and excellent choices where previously they went unnoticed and unacknowledged.

Keep in mind that this does not mean that we ignore the things that go wrong or the rules that are broken. There are consequences to be meted out in those circumstances, and you will learn how to handle this in chapters to come. But in order to create the foundation needed for consequences to truly work – consequences that basically amount to a "time-out" – you need to establish groundwork that consists of an inner-wealth-promoting, positive, success-laden *time-in*.

The time-in is the natural balance and complement to the time-out, our consequence of choice.

Some of you may roll your eyes at the mere mention of the time-out, thinking, *I've already tried that and it doesn't work*; or *yeah, right, watch me try to give my 'tween or teen a time-out and watch him laugh right in my face!* Bear with me – my approach takes a different tack that will work beautifully in the vast majority of instances. Besides: there is almost no consequence that is not, in essence, a time-out.

Having privileges revoked, doing extra chores, being grounded, or being sent to one's room are forms of "missing out" and are all time-outs. The trick is to find the version that works consistently.

You will come to see that no time-out can possibly work unless there is a time-in to miss out on. You will also come to see why most conventional time-outs are doomed to failure because they accidentally reward the problem. It will quickly become apparent that time-in holds so much more power and energy than time-out. Describing any "balance" between time-in and time-out is misleading. This imbalance (or inequality) between time-out and time-in is crucial for two aspects of this approach: to instill inner wealth, and to make the brief, un-energized consequences meaningful and effective. Time-out is a feather; time-in is a peacock!

The time-in is where children:

- Are actively accruing inner wealth;
- Have specific evidence that they are good inside;
- Come to feel that they have special meaning to themselves and to others;
- Feel as though they belong wherever they happen to be;
- Feel, in an overarching way, that they are "in the game" and that the game of life is exciting and captivating;
- Know that they are great participants in that game;
- Are confident that they are valuable to others; and
- Feel competent at managing their lives, relationships and feelings.

All of this is possible with this model because of the *specific kinds of appreciation, recognition and acknowledgment* children receive. Time-in is where the child's problems are given far less power and importance than the qualities of greatness she exhibits.

While in time-in, children find that their problems have little to no power over the positive focus of the adults around them. They find that the expectation of success is unshakable in the adults around them – *even as they are held to a high expectation of strict rule enforcement.*

They're surrounded by successes, and they feel ownership of these successes, which surround them like a minefield. They feel truly valued: like meaningful participants in the game of life. Their greatness becomes second nature – as dependable a part of their existence as the flow of their breath.

In the context of this rich time-in, problems mean only a brief time-out from relationship and access to what life has to offer, a brief moment to reset, or a brief transformation of relationship into something that holds far less energetic appeal than the time-in. Then, as soon as possible, typically in a matter of seconds, we jump with both feet into acknowledging the next success. This way we get to promote the awakening to greatness and to remain in the truth of the next moment when the rules are not being broken.

One of the best illustrations I've discovered of effective time-in and time-out comes from – of all things – video games.

"Video Game Therapy"

As your children's favorite toy, your power to guide your children toward experiences of success relies upon your ability to make your energetic features "pop" at the right times (when your child is showing aspects of himself that you wish to encourage), instead of the wrong times (when your child is making poor choices).

Believe it or not, video games – those sources of generous blood, gore, gratuitous violence and just plain inane content – are excellent teachers for us on this front. However, please don't interpret this as a recommendation in favor of video games! We're going to hijack the techniques game designers use to make those games so riveting and irresistible, and use them as a vessel for far more wonderful content.

Have you noticed how children who are normally hyperactive or otherwise challenging become captivated, motivated and accomplished when playing video games? So-called "normal" children also seem to thrive in these constructed environments. There's a good reason for this, and it's a great lesson for those who are seeking ways to help their child become equally captivated, motivated and accomplished in other areas of life.

Video Game Lesson: Clear Rules, Clear Consequences, and Right Back in the Game of Greatness

These games consume the attention of even very difficult children because **their lives make total sense while they are engaged in the game.** They are, in essence, enjoying a time-in as long as they're accruing points or moving toward the game's goals, reaching those goals and avoiding the pitfalls of violating the rules. If a rule is broken, they get a brief, un-energized consequence. Then, in the very next nano-second, it's right back to highly energized success. The clarity of it is hugely appealing to most children, but especially to "difficult" children – for whom adult expectations can be very *un*clear. Typically, the harder we try to be exceedingly clear, the more inadvertently unclear things get as we say we want one thing, but energize the exact opposite.

As they avoid danger or attain goals in the context of that game, the game confronts the child with profound evidence of success. Lots of energy transpires as they are immediately acknowledged and recognized with points, sounds, access to new levels or other landmarks of success. When they break a rule while playing the game, they get a clear, immediate, but not terribly interesting consequence. The game remains in the truth of the moment. The timing is always perfect. It all plays out in a predictable fashion.

Children figure this out in no time flat, and they see that there's no getting around the program. It's unflappable. It can't be bullied or manipulated. No amount of tantrums or pleading or nagging can change the format.

Even young children can figure out new video games in the time it would take most adults to locate the manual. Once they size the game up and assess that there's plenty of excitement and recognition for their wise and skillful actions and only a consequence for crossing the line, they throw themselves into performing at their top level. They don't waste their time trying to manipulate or bully the game; instead, they direct their intelligence into doing well.

If the video game exuded an energized display of sounds and colors and lights whenever points were lost, you can bet that kids would *try* to lose points, just to experience the fireworks. That would be as energetically upside-down as conventional techniques of parenting and teaching.

As heads roll and blood spurts in these games, parents might view certain video game consequences as extreme or even disturbing. But ask children who play violent video games whether they fear these consequences. To them, those consequences are literally nothing – because within seconds, they're back in the game, with more chances to score.

The child who is enjoying a video game is experiencing what it feels like to use her intensity in a successful manner. She is clearly, amply provided with evidence of her attainment and mastery and the excitement associated with success. And she can count on this every time she sits down to play. She comes to love manifesting her greatness within that framework of clarity. She keeps wanting to climb the ladder of greater levels of possibilities.

What would you give to see your children involve themselves in school life and home life in this way – investing and focusing their energies in increasingly successful ways, without the benefit of parental pressures, lectures, warnings or exhortations…following the rules of their own volition, without urging or coercion?

Here's the key. Video games have a structure within which children feel immensely secure. There is an abundance of acknowledgment in the form of audible "bells and whistles" and discernible, continuous scoring in response to the child's positive accomplishments – even in response to steps *toward* those accomplishments. Consequences are reflected in completely straightforward ways, clearly, predictably and immediately, with no bells or whistles; but when the consequence is over, the child gets right back to new opportunities to score. The consequence is not feared by the child; he just renews his efforts and determination to score more points.

The child has what amounts to an *illusion* of a result, but that illusion is powerful and influential. The same relationship exists between time-out and time-in: following a consequence that amounts to a "reset," the child can't wait to have access to success again.

Most children also thrive in the context of athletics, too, and this has to do with the clarity of the lines drawn between success and rule-breaking. When a child succeeds, she gets cheered by her teammates or the crowd and perhaps sees her team earn points. When she breaks a rule, she knows that there will be a consequence, and she knows what it will be.

The referee doesn't yell or scream at players who step outside the boundaries of the game's rules. He simply states the consequence neutrally, holding the player fully accountable. The player takes responsibility and no excitement or energy is given to the broken rule. There is just a clear result. This structure consistently brings out the best that athletes have to give. Even athletes who seem barely able to conduct themselves off the playing field without creating havoc seem to thrive within the structured parameters of the game. A toe on the line is a toe on the line, and when the simple consequence is over, the player is right back in the game.

Athletics awaken children to the excitement of achievement and the sense of fulfillment that comes from success. In sports, failure holds no excitement. Unfortunately, for so many children who accidentally get energized for their problems, this does not tend to be the case in real life.

Most parents are less than thrilled by the subject matter of most video games, and others may disdain the competition or danger that can be involved in sports programs for children. But regardless of how you may feel about video games or children's sports, know this: *We can observe, learn and apply their underlying principles to parenting our children away from failures and toward new patterns of success.*

The basic translation is:

- **Energy, response and relationship for the good stuff**
- **"Oops, broke a rule, here's your consequence" with no energy, reaction or payoff for violations**

Following through with this intention requires that rules be extremely clear and that consequences are delivered with total consistency. More on that in the next chapter.

Once the player has been held accountable in a clean, un-energized fashion, it's right back to the excitement of participation and success. This is always the case, every time the game is played. The game defaults to inferences of greatness. All the child seems to want to do is play that out, to higher and higher levels of attainment.

Teach the lessons when the lessons can be imbedded in successes; avoid teaching through problems, when the child is least receptive.

That's easier to do than most people think. The techniques in this book will give you the tools you require. The structure is simple – a sensible blend of recognition and limits. It allows for a beautiful outcome of mastery and accomplishment for the child through clear rules, consistently enforced, with a great time-in always the default.

Let's review the four underlying concepts we've examined so far – concepts the Nurtured Heart Approach uses to propel the intention of manifesting greatness:

1. **We Are Our Child's Favorite Toys**
   ...making the right features "pop" at the right time will draw children inexorably into success.

2. **Shamu: Catching Goodness vs. Creating Goodness**
   ...take every opportunity to create successes that would otherwise not exist.

3. **Toll-taker: Choosing the Way We See Things**
   ...take a "snapshot" of this moment and see, appreciate and acknowledge the greatness that is always there – created by our willingness to choose to see it.

4. **Video Game Theory: Clear Rules, Clear Consequences and Right Back in the Game of Greatness**
   ..."Oops, broke a rule, here's your consequence" when a rule is broken; no additional energy, reaction or payoff for violations. All the energized response comes when the rules ARE NOT being broken. That's the default setting.

Finding Better Buttons

Many parents intuitively get the video game connection, aptly describing their child's limit-pushing: "He really knows how to push my buttons." We all have buttons – particular behaviors that are especially frustrating or annoying to us. Some of us openly advertise where those buttons are and exactly what it takes to push them. Kids are extremely skilled at finding them, even when we do our best to hide them away. **But there are ways to create better buttons!**

When our children are feeling especially needy, sensitive or energized, they can dial into our reactions by manifesting particular behaviors that they know, from years of experience, will get us going.

Adults are particularly vulnerable when stressed or distracted. The child takes note that we are "unavailable" unless he starts pushing buttons like mad. (What parent hasn't had the experience of trying to conduct important business on the phone while being hounded by a needy young child?)

Under those circumstances, you might as well wear a neon sign declaring to the child that the only way parental involvement is available is through extracting a response. Even if the reaction is a negative one, to a child who is feeling needy, any response is better than no response at all. In the way things add up for a child, any response can feel like intimacy. The charged closeness that comes through adversity can be experienced as a strong, satisfying connection, albeit a negative one.

Impressions evolve into patterns; a child can quickly move into a place where he finds himself pushing your buttons constantly without the slightest understanding of why he's doing it. He is simply acting in a manner that consistently replicates strong connections. Adults do the same thing; think back to the last time you started an argument with your spouse or other loved one, only to realize later that you did so because you felt disconnected and needed to re-establish intimacy. Most of us learned this habit as very young children.

The negative button-pushing will go on unless we can demonstrate, to the child's satisfaction, that the payoffs are substantially greater for the good stuff. We show that through the ways in which we choose to give our energies.

We must create a new perception – the perception that we, as toys or as the child's "entertainment center," radiate greater responses:

1. when challenging behaviors are *not* happening, *and*
2. when successful behaviors *are* happening.

And then, to amp the whole thing up and make it irresistible to the child, we add the element of greatness. We move the child into a higher-order realm that goes beyond simple "goodness" or absence of problems.

We have to be convincing, and so we need to learn to see success in a whole new way. We need to learn to literally *hijack* the child into success and not just give lip service and pep talks.

Kids have superlative abilities to detect when we are insincere or superficial, so we have to demonstrate that we truly feel and radiate authentic excitement, animation and energy in response to everything that is *not* a problem. You will see that accomplishing this through first-hand experiences is actually a piece of cake.

Break It Down and Add It Up

How do we see successes where it seems there are none? How do we find abundant, specific examples of success in simple daily acts? This requires a paradigm shift: (1) a willingness to see the good in each moment, starting with the present moment, and letting go of every previous and future moment, like the attitude of the dancing toll-taker; and (2) the mindset to make success unavoidable, like Shamu's trainers did.

To accomplish this paradigm shift, we must develop the insight to break down the most mundane day-to-day activities into abundant examples of success. I will illustrate this with a real-life example (created by Nurtured Heart Approach instructor and therapist Tom Grove).

The Pencil Sharpener: An Instructive Tale

Let's take an ordinary task – a student sharpening a pencil before class – and break it down into many elements or steps.

First of all, he has to remember that he needs a pencil. He has to keep track of it and be aware of its dull condition – or, perhaps, he has the discipline to remember to sharpen before class no matter what shape the pencil is in. He has to keep track of time to get his pencil sharpened before class period begins. Maybe he doesn't remember to sharpen at first but has the awareness of what others are doing and takes a cue from them. If there's a line, he needs to be able to take turns. He must gauge how long the pencil needs to be in the sharpener to get it just right and not grind it down too far or make the point too delicate. He needs to get to the sharpener and back without incident or commotion. Before going over there in the first place, he has to make sure it is the pencil he really wants to use.

Such a multitude of acts might result from good planning, forethought, a good memory, being considerate of others, remembering the rules, paying attention to time, keeping track of important things, choosing to be a ready learner, being able to choose what is important, and so on. See how many ways a simple task like sharpening a pencil can be broken down? Every one of those thoughts and steps the child took can be used as an opportunity to recognize success and even greatness.

The next time you think you couldn't possibly find a way to praise your child – the one who just can't seem to get anything right – remember the pencil sharpener. Break his actions into these same kinds of tiny choices and decisions, and you'll find plenty to celebrate!

Begin to break down your child's choices in the same way we've broken down a trip to the pencil sharpener. See how they reflect some quality of success and accomplishment that comprises our sense of inner wealth. "Good job" doesn't come close in energy or specificity to acknowledging the multitude of talents, choices and self-control shown by the child sharpening the pencil – or the child who just does what's required every day.

Another example: the child who brushes his teeth before bed. He is remembering that it's important to keep his teeth clean. He has to know where his toothbrush is kept and to deposit just the right amount of toothpaste on it. He has to cooperate with siblings who also need to brush their teeth at the same sink. He has to remember to wet the toothbrush and toothpaste before brushing, and then he has to use the technique the dentist demonstrated to get all the "sugar bugs" off of every one of his teeth and to rinse his mouth afterwards, being careful not to swallow any toothpaste. Finally, he has to remember to rinse his brush and put everything back where it goes; wipe the toothpaste foam from around his mouth; hang the towel back on its hook; and turn the bathroom light out as he leaves.

You have a choice. You can clearly take all these actions for granted. After all, brushing is a task that simply needs to get done, so why fuss about it? On the flip side, think of how verbally annoyed you can get when your child refuses to brush or is remiss in any part of the process.

Think how much you would have to say – probably, with great animation and emotion – if that were the case. Why not proactively appreciate and acknowledge your child's every positive choice on the path to clean teeth? If you wouldn't hesitate to tell the truth vehemently if things go wrong, why not choose to tell the detailed truth of what's going right – when expensive cavities aren't happening?

A few ideas of how you might energize this everyday task:

- Alex, I really appreciate that you cleaned up after you brushed and did it so carefully. That shows me how thoughtful you are. You didn't leave it for me to do. That is being a helpful and great person.
- Jesse, I notice that you followed the dentist's directions when you brushed tonight. That shows me you listened carefully and that you care about the health of your teeth. I really am grateful that you are being responsible in this way.
- Dana, I really like how you shared the sink with your brother when you two were brushing. You could have fooled around and made a mess but you didn't, and I really like the respect you are showing one another. Respect is a quality of greatness that I see in you.

When we break the child's actions down in this way, we can see how to celebrate children for "just doing what they're supposed to do." Whatever they are doing, they are displaying abundant talents and qualities that can be worthy of praise. All we have to do is notice whatís in front of us and hold the right mindset to feed back to them, in clear and exciting language, all the wonderful aspects of their steps toward success.

Not a More Time-Consuming Approach

At this point, you might be thinking, "Who has time for this stuff? It's all I can do to get everything done in a day – and now I'm supposed to take all this time and acknowledge my kid whenever he's NOT screwing up?"

After years and years of teaching the Nurtured Heart Approach and observing how parents learn to apply it, I can assure you that you need not fear that this will be overly time-consuming. In the very beginning, it will require more of your attention and effort, just as with any new endeavor, but consider what is at stake. Imagine that you are trying to start and sustain a campfire on a cold, wet evening. Imagine all the extra effort necessary to find the kindling dry enough to get something going, and then the concentration and determination necessary to get the fire to move from twig to twig to twig. The process of growing inner wealth in a child is equally painstaking in the earliest stages. Even though the twig stage is protracted and you have to be patient enough to wait to toss in a big log, you will soon be rewarded with a raging, toasty fire even on a cold, rainy night. At that point, the fire truly has a life of its own. Safely contained, the fire can now even easily overcome wet wood.

The time and energy required by you to keep fostering inner wealth in your child will be significantly less than you might otherwise expend on lectures, warnings and punishments. Even in the start-up phase, as you begin to implement the Nurtured Heart Approach, **giving as many compliments as I recommend should take less than five minutes a day.**

At times when things are not going well, think of all the time you spend discussing problems, issuing warnings, giving lectures or raising your voice in reprimands…all the time spent agonizing over how to deal with misbehavior and the effort required to enforce punishments. Once you master the art of precise, colorful, energized acknowledgement, you'll more than likely find that this initial period of investing extra time will lead you to a place where discipline will take considerably less time and energy than before. And the end result – a transformed child – will be more than worth it.

Improving Relationship Language

Most children, like most adults, know how to recognize success at the "good job" or "thank you" level. This is how they've been recognized. Most believe that, unless they are doing something spectacular or at least above and beyond, they won't get more exciting feedback from those around them; and they believe that others don't deserve such feedback unless *they're* doing something spectacular. Self-esteem evaporates as some children surrender themselves to the idea that they won't ever do anything well enough or achieve highly enough to earn truly inspiring feedback from adults and peers.

This happens more than you think, especially in school settings. Some at-risk kids end up acting out and causing trouble so that they can get richer, more colorful responses; others quietly crave those responses and don't know how to get them, or even what they'd sound like if they *did* get them.

Some children develop anxious or depressed responses to the world as they give up on the possibility of inspired connection through "being good." They begin to explore the vast menu of ways to obtain that connection through negativity.

As you begin to use the new, engaging language of the Nurtured Heart Approach, you'll find that the children in your life will begin to develop creative language and feedback systems that help them recognize and verbally express "great person." In other words: You will be instilling inner wealth in your child through your inspired appreciativeness, and at the same time, you'll be teaching him how to do the same for others.

Where once there was only "good job" and "thanks for doing that," there will be language that's up to the task of introducing children and adults to the wonderful qualities they possess, to the essence of who they really are, in great detail. This is accomplished by holding up the mirror to the child and clearly reflecting his success, intertwining appreciation with aspects of greatness. As inner wealth expands, so does the child's ability to be in healthy relationship with others.

We can awaken to the good in each moment; and, by doing so, awaken the child to the good in himself and in others. Sure, the child might forget to sharpen his pencil at first, or he might break the point during the first attempt, but these problems quickly give way to the next success, and we can be right there to acknowledge that. There are abundant successes to be seen and recognized in each moment of progress.

This kind of recognition is equivalent to rewarding Shamu for aiming toward the rope, being in the right area, looking at the rope, swimming at the right speed – any factor that might lead him to actually pass over it. As Nurtured Heart trainer Tom Grove likes to say: *If you want Shamu to swim over the rope and he almost never does, put rope everywhere!*

Here are some words you can substitute for "thank you" and "good job." I recommend that you photocopy this and refer to it often as you read through the next chapters and start to develop this new way of recognizing, appreciating and creating greatness in your child.

As you acknowledge your child, experiment with the addition of a few extra words that explain what inspired you to provide this recognition. This will make your positive influence even more powerful.

Tell the child that he or she is...

A joy	Admirable
A good friend	Appreciative
A hard worker	Attentive
A source of strength	Attentive to detail
A leader	Being dazzling
A light	Being inspiring
A lighthouse	Being surprising
A helper	Being powerful
A scientist	Being wise
A great example	Brave
An advocate	Bringing out the best in others
Aware	Being inspiring
Accomplishing a lot	Beaming
Acting creatively	Choosing what's important
Acting spirited	Compassionate

Considerate
Cooperative
Creative
Courageous
Constructive
Clear
Clear-minded
Committed
Courteous
Dedicated to success
Diligent
Discerning
Direct
Dignified
Deeply understanding
Demonstrating integrity
Exceeding expectations
Easy to like
Efficient
Empathetic
Expansive
Feeling the joy of discovery
Flashing a contagious smile
Finding new in the ordinary
Faithful
Focused
Forgiving
Generous
Going above and beyond
Gracious
Genuine
Good-hearted
Glorious
Having unique ideas
Having great curiosity
Handling strong emotions well
Having an open mind

Honorable
Hopeful
Independent
Inspiring
Inquisitive
Intelligent
Possessing innate ability
Just and fair
Kind
Loving
Looking out for others
Managing his/her time well
Making a happy mood
Making a hard task look easy
Making great choices
Making an insightful inference
Making delightful deductions
Making a solid educated guess
Organized
Open-minded
Pulling together
Patient
Positive
Peaceable
Powerfully spirited
Productive
Passionate
Reasonable
Respectful
Respecting self
Refined
Responsible
Seeing the big picture
Self-controlled
Sunshine to others
Steadfast
Strong on the inside

Trustworthy
Thankful
Thrifty
Tactful
Thoughtful
Understanding
Using a pleasant voice
Using your great mind
Vibrant
Visionary

Or that he or she *has...*
A quick mind
Brilliant thoughts
A pleasant manner
A fine sense of humor
A wonderful sense of beauty
A great appreciation of art
A great sense of logic
A great ability to be receptive

**Or that he or she is *showing,
having,* or *demonstrating...***
Amazing forethought
Balanced thinking
Excellent planning skills
Good teamwork
Imagination
Knowledge of when to reflect
Magnificent thinking
Perseverance
Real talent
That she/he has been
raised right
Zest

**Add your own inspired
appreciations here...**

PART TWO: PARENT'S GUIDE TO THE NURTURED HEART APPROACH

There is nothing which the soul cannot know, for the whole objective existence is made by the soul for its own use, and therefore it is not astonishing if man possesses great qualities that he has not inherited…if he has knowledge of all things through revelation, not by learning. It is astonishing only when he lacks this, and that is owing to the globes upon globes of the objective world covering the light of the soul.
– Hazrat Inyat Khan

Run away from greatness and greatness will follow you.
– Abu Bakr

CHAPTER FIVE

The Stands and the Methods

Imagine yourself going into your child's room to deliver a pile of clean, folded laundry. Look around. If it's like most children's rooms, there are quite a few items out of place: Plenty that needs to be done; plenty that hasn't been done despite your requests; and plenty that was done halfheartedly and could have been done better.

It's our usual game of "what's wrong with this picture?" Depending upon your need for the child's room to be just so, this may bring up some major ire for you and may serve as a source of conflict between you and your child.

Now, put yourself back into the same room. How adept are you at seeing what is right? Typically, something must be far more than minutely good before it becomes a big enough blip on the parental radar screen to merit comment. We may commend a child for a noticeable act of respect or responsibility, but we are *much less* likely to comment on smaller instances…if we notice them at all.

Hundreds or thousands of years ago, humans had to be extremely alert to danger. They couldn't just wait until danger was upon them; they had to sense around corners, use and trust their instincts, and apply their senses constantly in an effort to detect danger before it got the best of them. Here's what Martin Seligman, the first psychiatrist to devote himself to academic study of positive psychology, says on this subject:

> Because our brain evolved during a time of ice, flood and famine, we have a catastrophic brain. The way the brain works is looking for what's wrong. The problem is, that worked in the Pleistocene era…but it doesn't work in the modern world.

In this context, our attention to what's wrong makes perfect biological sense. As descendants of ancestors who had to develop sophisticated abilities to sniff and scout out danger, we carry in our genetic makeup built-in detectors of all that is wrong or potentially wrong, along with built-in reactivity. We wouldn't be here if our ancestors weren't good enough at this to have survived.

Seeing what's right hasn't been a survival skill as of yet. My contention is that it is becoming a skill that may not literally be essential for individual survival, but required for our long-term survival and happiness as a species...and for the long-term preservation of all that is important to us.

The ability to zero in on what's going right – the linchpin of the Nurtured Heart Approach – has to be cultivated by conscious effort until it becomes second nature. The good news is that the child whose parents expose him to this will pick it up right away, and if it's done consistently, he'll do it as effortlessly as most of us now hone in on what's wrong with the world. This kind of evolution is much quicker than Darwin's version – potentially, it can happen in a single generation.

Opportunities to see goodness and right choices are everywhere, in every moment. If we can become conscious enough to create a frame of "great person! succeeding person!" for our children in 30 or 20 or even 10 of those several thousand fleeting moments that make up each day, we can have enormous impact.

As parents, we jump into that window of opportunity and use a few powerful techniques that reflect to the child, "Here you are being successful...here's a quality of your greatness...and here's what I mean by that." Or "Here's what you're *not* doing, and here's how that makes you successful, too."

In this chapter, you will learn the basic methods of the approach and the stands upon which they're based. The stands are core concepts to which you can return when you find yourself missing the mark – or wanting to ramp up your impact.

First, let's look at the stands that support the methods – the "commandments" that give the techniques their power. When you reach the four main techniques used in the Nurtured Heart Approach, I encourage you to start applying each technique on its own before going on to read about the next one.

The Stands

The Nurtured Heart Approach is founded on three stands. Each stand is supported by the four underlying concepts described in the previous chapter. The stands essentially are the "commandments" of this way of parenting or, if you prefer, of this social curriculum. As you move forward into the actual techniques, I'll remind you periodically of the relevance of the stands and their underlying concepts to foster your grasp of each technique.

Like any commandment, these get broken from time to time. The key is not perfect execution (no one does that, not even me!) but to use the stands as motivation or as guideposts to help you get back on track in the next moments.

You can picture these three stands as a "three-legged table." Keep all three legs in place and your table won't topple. And if you see it wobbling, act quickly to get it steady once again.

Stand I: The relentless pursuit and celebration of positivity.

Resolve to purposefully create and nurture successes and greatness; relentlessly and strategically draw children into new and renewed patterns of success and greatness.

The recognition techniques outlined later in this chapter are the tools you'll use to do this. It's time. Why not now? Why not conspire to bring out the greatness that lies within every human being?

Stand II: Strict rule enforcement.

Resolve to have (1) clear rules and (2) clear, consistent, effective consequences when those rules are broken.

We won't be looking the other way if we see or sense a rule being broken and we will provide a consistent yet effective consequence that is easy to administer.

We do this in two ways: first, by couching rules in extremely clear *negative* language. That's right, *negative*. Rules are the place to use negative language so that the child knows exactly where the boundary lies between a followed rule and a broken rule. Positive rules make it hard to discern when a line has been crossed. They inevitably lead to too many warnings – warnings that keep energizing the same issues we are trying to solve.

For example, instead of the rule "use good manners," the rule should be "No interrupting,'" or "No talking with your mouth full," or an overarching "No bad manners." Instead of a rule that says, "Be nice to each other," make it, "No hitting. No arguing. No grabbing things from others' hands. No taking your brother's belongings without asking."

Rules are about what the child should *not* do. This makes it extremely clear for the child and there's no more room to maneuver or manipulate, which children are wont to do. It is advantageous to parents, too, as these kinds of rules give you all the more "pencil sharpener" observations (flip back to the previous chapter if you need a refresher on this concept) to use when positively reinforcing your child. **You can build a wonderful sense of success and inner wealth when you give the child positive reflections whenever she is not breaking a rule.**

The second part of strict rule enforcement is, obviously, the enforcement. Commit to always delivering a consequence when a rule is broken: no negotiation, no warnings, no waffling, no lectures or lengthy diatribes. Think of the video game theory: Clarity of rules and consequences, with a brief, un-energized time-out, are all that's needed to get the child back in the game. Consequences must be clear, predictable, consistent, and always followed through.

You cannot enforce a limit unless that line is drawn and the limit set. If it is unclear, one never really knows when the limit is violated. Once you have total clarity on those limits, you can teach the child where he is by applauding him when he chooses not to break the rules.

Teach rules through enforcing them when they're broken   and by pointing out times in which they are *not* being broken. If you find yourself repeating a rule, it's time to start enforcing it. If you don't enforce it every time, it isn't a rule. If you find yourself thinking, "These kids have forgotten the rules," you probably need to be stricter in your enforcement of those rules – and you probably also need to amp up your celebration and recognition of rules *not* broken, pointing out even the smallest degrees of appropriate effort, attitude and action.

To create consequences that actually work, it is necessary to set a firm and broad foundation of positivity and success (time-in) that becomes the norm in your child's daily life. We use a clean time-out/ reset for consequences; the methods for doing this are not complex, but very specific, and so I've devoted a whole chapter to this subject. **For now, just keep in mind that establishing the time-in is what makes a brief, clean time-out work so beautifully.**

Stand III: Not leaking negativity.
Resolve to NOT get drawn into giving the child greater responses, more animation and other unintended "payoffs" for negative behaviors. Avoid, at all costs, accidentally fostering failures and rewarding problems with your energy, response and relationship. No more $100 bills for problems.

It isn't unusual for children to resist initial application of the approach's methods. Your new language will probably strike them as weird. They may disagree with your observations. You may be tempted to revert to old methods – lectures, escalating consequences, warnings, instilling fear, threatening to take away something the child values – in order to try to get the child in line.

This is what we call *leaking negativity.* It undermines the effectiveness of the approach by defusing the solidity of the child's emerging inner wealth. If leaking is significant, no matter how stunning the new move to greatness, the adult ultimately will struggle to create the level of time-in that is needed to make the time-out work optimally as a consequence. You may still see some level of improvement but the transformational level of change that this approach is about will not be reached.

However – and this is an important point – **leaking negativity is something that we** *all* **do;** the goal is to do it less, to catch ourselves doing it, and to stop that leak in the next brand-new, possibility-full moment.

A leak of negativity is an action or statement that demonstrates to the child:

- that problems, issues, and broken rules captivate and elicit your charged interest
- your expectation that the child will do something wrong
- your willingness to focus energy and attention on poor choices
- the child's ability to access the "buttons" that make your features pop by making poor choices or breaking rules
- that relationship and "love" flow more strongly as a result of the child doing something less than acceptable, so that the child perceives, at a deep, subconscious level, that more love is available in response to wrong behavior

One of the best aspects of the Nurtured Heart Approach is the fact that it does not require perfect execution on the part of the parent. You can really just dive in, play around with it, and even leak negative energy and still come out with the most wonderful results...as long as you stay in the moment and keep applying and refining your version of the approach. See the leaks, plug them up, and move on.

Everyone who uses this approach will leak negativity; we all have bad days and we all slip up. But because the method is founded on staying in each moment, you simply move from the last moment into this one with a clean slate and keep on trying.

Nothing but Moments

If you allowed us to film your life yesterday and play parts of it today, we could play that footage back in numerous ways. We could play it in fast-forward or we could play it at regular speed. We could also play it in a frame-by-frame mode. And if we did the latter, we could watch those frames in a few different ways. We could watch silently, or we could watch and critique each frame...or we could watch and celebrate each frame.

For most of us, it would be much easier to find five ways to criticize what's depicted in each frame – what could have been done better or what wasn't done that should have been done – than to find five distinct, detailed ways to *celebrate* each frame…to describe ways in which it shows you being successful. Let's look at four techniques, each of which builds on the one before it, that will give you the tools to help you celebrate instead of criticize.

The Methods: Strategies to Support the Stands

Active Recognition
Video Moments

Experiential Recognition
Teaching Values through Experience

Proactive Recognition
Celebrating Children for Not Breaking Rules

Creative Recognition
Hijacking Children into Success

Active Recognition (or Video Moments)

Clearly Observing What the Child Is Doing:

This first strategy I call Active Recognition. It is the first stage of relentlessly pursuing positivity. You are simply offering the child a "verbal snapshot" of what you see her doing: no judgment or evaluation, simply detailed observation. For example:

"I see that you are using red, yellow and green yarn to make your weaving."

"I can hear that you and your other group members are collaborating on your homework project."

"I see that you're really angry right now and I see that you are handling your feelings beautifully."

In this technique, we simply take a "verbal snapshot" of the child. We show her she's not invisible, even when she's not acting-out. We irrefutably demonstrate that she's really *seen,* whether she's engaged in exemplary or ordinary behavior. I often refer to Active Recognition as "Video Moments," because in those moments, we simply reflect to the child exactly what we see, exactly what the lens registers, without any kind of evaluation or judgment.

Simply say, out loud, what you see the child doing, almost as though you were describing it to a blind person. **Only use it when the child is doing something positive. Never do it when you see the child doing wrong.**

When you use this technique, the child feels that she is irrefutably *seen, acknowledged* and *appreciated.* On your end, it helps you be more attuned to noticing when the child is succeeding. For the child who is desperate to be noticed, recognition of his everyday actions, feelings and expressions help anchor him in the belief that his life really matters. It develops a foundation of trust.

Think of it this way: We're trying to alter the wiring in the child that draws him toward negativity by activating new circuitry of positivity. To change that wiring, we have to access the wire box. This first technique is the tool we use to do that.

Creating successes that wouldn't otherwise exist and having them register within the child in an irrefutable way are especially important for the child who doesn't yet trust positive statements – especially if he currently experiences himself as someone who receives more energy and relationship by getting in trouble.

Some children have accumulated first-hand experiences of failure, driven home by remarks intended to set limits: "don't do that" or "cut that out," for example. No matter how well-intended these comments, no matter how lovingly offered, children who are recipients of remarks like these will often feel them as tinged with criticism. This view comes to comprise the truth of whom the child feels she is in that moment (unless she has sufficient inner wealth). Just as any adult might reject a compliment on how he looks on a day when he doesn't feel he looks good, the child with a deep belief that he is "not good" won't exactly drink in statements to the contrary unless those statements are designed to be powerful and irrefutable. We need a way to get around that defensiveness, and video moments (or Active Recognitions) are the beginning of this process – especially because they are embedded in first-hand experiences that ring true in the child's bones, so to speak.

My favorite example of how *not* to do this is the typical adult response to a child's drawing. Usually, it's a variation of "What a beautiful picture," or "I love your picture." Instead, the Active Recognition technique recommends that the adult simply describe what is actually in the picture or what is taking place in the moment. No judgment, no technical critique – nothing that can be perceived as criticism at all. You'll be astonished to see how beautifully most children respond to this. They know that they have been truly seen and acknowledged. The detail makes it irrefutable.

The child feels in her bones that she is being held in esteem. She experiences, at the cellular level, that she is worthy of someone's time, just in doing what she normally does in the course of a day. She doesn't have to be doing something spectacular. This allows a parent or teacher to help a child feel loved and cherished just the way she is.

When applying this technique:

- **Use neutral, non-judgmental language to make the message as "digestible" as possible.** Some children will rankle or resist when you suddenly begin noticing them in unusual ways. Your way around this is to start out without actually giving glowing recognition; just observe and report. There's no arguing with or denying direct observations of what the child is doing or being in the moment.

- **Be as specific as possible; give lots of information.** You can say "good job" or "thank you" or "that's beautiful" with all the emotion in the world, but the child isn't going to know exactly what you mean unless you are specific. Detail makes recognition convincing to the child and helps her feel cherished and validated. Active Recognition gives you a chance to practice being detailed in your observations in the moment, before adding the element of appreciation later on.

An Active Recognition is like a photographic opportunity to capture a moment, just the way a camera does, and to tell the truth of that moment. As you build to the other techniques, you'll learn to relay that "snapshot" back to the child verbally in a way that conveys to the child that he has been successful and that he is held in esteem and worthy of your time.

Examples: Active Recognition

"Jo, I see that you are building a tower with colored blocks and you are being extremely careful as you place them to keep the tower balanced."

"Paul, I can tell that you are eager to go outside and play!"

"Erin, you're gluing colored paper scraps to your project. I see pink, purple and green scraps in your pile and you're connecting them at all kinds of interesting angles."

You can use active recognition/video moments to redirect a child before a rule is broken:

"Jenny, I can see that you are feeling frustrated right now and you're not taking it out on anyone."

"I see that you're bored and restless right now, Thomas, and you seem to be looking for something new to do."

Do <u>not</u>, however, use this method once the child has crossed the line. If Jenny lashes out at her sister, or if Thomas digs into the stereo equipment with a screwdriver, it's consequence time.

Use voice modulations to put more "oomph" into your video moments.

And don't hesitate to try video moments with all of the people in your life: spouse, co-workers or friends. It's good practice, and you'll be surprised to see how this kind of acknowledgement starts wonderful conversations and helps the people in your life feel connected to you.

If your children respond negatively to this new kind of attention, don't get sucked into that negativity. For example, if your child tells you, "Stop saying these things. Leave me alone. What did you do, read another dumb parenting book?" **Remember that you are taking a stand.** Try saying something like this that uses more of this same technique but doesn't back off:

"I can tell you are noticing that I'm doing something different and I appreciate that you are letting me know without arguing. And yes, I *have* read another parenting book. I realized I've been focusing a lot on what you do wrong. I'm starting to try to see all the very many things you do that are right! It's new and different for me as well and maybe we'll both eventually get used to it."

I can't overstate the importance of keeping your stand of creating a new world of successfulness. The tragedy would be to fear the confrontation and go searching for yet another approach.

You may find your children acting out at first as they begin to receive your recognitions. Interpret this as a sign that they are enjoying the positive connection, but they're still trying to get you to respond to them through their old button-pushing techniques. They want to make the connection last, and acting out is their tried-and-true method for that. Give them time to come around – to begin to trust success as much as they used to trust negativity. Don't energize their negativity; withdraw relationship when the child makes poor choices by giving an un-energized time-out. (I'll cover this in detail in Chapter 6; feel free to peek ahead to get the fundamentals right now.)

Why wait for the wheels to come off? Jump in and breathe your nurturing energy into your child by using your "camera" *before* a rule gets broken: "I see you getting frustrated and see you being smart by taking a break and walking off your feelings."

This is far more effective than warnings ("If you _____, I'm going to have to _____!!!" or "Don't you dare _____!"), which are basically an embossed invitation to the child to push your buttons and extract your precious relationship and energy. In our society, we think of warnings as an act of compassion. From an energetic point of view, however, warnings are ill-timed rewards: more $100 bills flowing at the wrong moments.

Practice Active Recognition for a few days, until it feels natural and your child accepts it as part of your interactions. Then, move to the next technique to continue expanding your inner wealth-building vocabulary.

Using Active Recognition to Support Healthy Expression of Emotions
Most adults can recall being told, as a child, "Stop crying!" or "Stop acting so angry, no one did anything to you!" This is especially true of men, many of whom find themselves completely unable to cry or to express/experience sadness, having been shamed for doing so as children. In some cases, these messages weren't spoken, but there was the distinct feeling that strong emotions were inconvenient, unwelcome or even shameful. It's time to break that pattern – to hand down to our children an acceptance and encouragement of their feeling, emotional selves.

If a child has sufficient inner wealth to allow strong emotions to come and go instead of stagnating or being "stuffed" because of an impression that they are "bad," emotions are valuable barometers and compasses that help children live their lives with integrity.

Every time a child perceives that he is wrong for having an emotional response to something, he becomes further removed from his feelings and his life force. Even asking a child to talk about what he is feeling can meet with defensiveness or the inability to truly explain; this further contributes to a sense of inadequacy with regard to emotions.

Even if the child did know what was bothering him, what are the chances of his putting it into words in a way that would make things "better"? Defining and talking about emotions and feelings do not always make it all better. If anything, putting words to emotions and feelings can separate us from the experience of having and being in touch with them as we try to organize the whole potentially messy business.

Being frightened of one's feelings can contribute to a great loss of vitality and life force. Anyone who fits this description is at risk for depression: the result of emotions and feelings that have not been allowed to run their course, but instead are literally *depressed,* compressed, squashed down. This may even cause one to subconsciously lash out at others.

I recommend practicing Active Recognition when your child becomes emotional about something. Don't wait until the emotion passes or becomes problematic. Make that emotional moment into a success: "Billy, I see that you are upset that I said you couldn't have dessert. I love that you are allowing yourself to feel your feelings and not taking your anger out on anybody."

You are saying to the child: *You are being successful by handling your strong feelings well.* This then translates to the child the feeling that he is someone who *can* handle strong feelings well – there's no question of whether he can or can't, *he is.* This helps the child in owning – even enjoying – his emotions.

One mother I know has worked on this concept since her children were very young, encouraging them to not shy away from strong emotions and to express them verbally if they can. She and her partner have made an effort to "video moment" strong emotions when they come up in their children and in themselves. At this writing, her four-year-old son can often be heard stating passionately, "I'm so ANGRY!" instead of hitting, pushing or engaging in other typical four-year-old behaviors. And every time he does this, he receives a shower of positive recognition for his healthy expression.

Building Greatness with Active Recognition
This is the first of several sections meant to illustrate ways in which the techniques can be "amped" to cultivate greatness.

When you use Active Recognition in the moments when your child is swept up in intense emotion, she gains insight into the greatness of that human quality: That although they can be hard, her emotions are great friends that will reveal to her difficult but crucial truths...that she can handle them wisely and powerfully...and that they don't need to be fixed or suppressed. Her response to her own emotions won't be to look for someone to rescue her from them – and she'll be protected from others victimizing her in vulnerable moments.

The child comes to feel that he doesn't have to go to the trouble of jumping through major hoops to deserve a sense of greatness. Recognition comes for successes large and small, precluding the need to jump ever higher (or choose increasingly intense rule-breaking behaviors) to get noticed. The child can relax into his life and trust that he will be deservedly noticed for ordinary events. The internal equivalent is that he will be at peace with himself. He will be able to give due notice to the important positive details of his life without having to go to extremes to get recognition or attention or closeness.

Below are examples of how Video Moments can be employed to introduce a child to his qualities of greatness. Many of the examples below pertain to moments when challenging emotions were emerging and the greatness contained in the choices to handle those well. However, greatness can be added to the whole range of Video Moments, well beyond the examples provided below:

"Tom, I saw how those kids were annoying you and how you chose to not give them any energy. And I also can tell you are frustrated, and you are handling that strong feeling well. I really appreciate how powerful you are being, not taking your anger out on those kids or anyone else. That power is a great quality you have."

"Marsha, I can see that the library dedication ceremony made you so excited and happy. I love that you give yourself the gift of being so open with your feelings. Being that open is such a great quality."

"Warren, I love how you handled your boredom earlier at Uncle Jim's house. That's not the easiest thing to hear him yapping on and on about his new business. Boredom can be pretty overwhelming and it's a pretty strong feeling. I appreciate how great you were in being respectful and kind."

"Adrienne, I know all that red tape and paperwork makes you mad and I loved seeing how determined you were to just plow through it. It looked like you used your anger to motivate you to just get it over and done. Tapping into the energy of your emotions is a great quality you have."

"Bob, I noticed you wiping down the counter after dinner. I know it's your job, but I just really appreciate that you do this so well and take it seriously and hardly ever need to be reminded. Your helpfulness is a quality of greatness that I admire in you."

"Dylan, I see that you're getting focused on your homework. I can see your determination to finish it and to do your best. That determination is a great quality that will get you far in life."

Experiential Recognition
Teaching Values through Experience:

If you saw a group of children who were cooperating well and asked how they were being wonderful, what would they say? Most likely, it would not be "We're being respectful and considerate!" These are abstractions, and children rarely think of their experiences in abstract terms. They might say, "We're playing nicely," but a great many behaviors go into broad concepts like "playing nicely." To promote their ability to live those concepts, including respect and consideration of others, they need us to link what they are doing (active recognition/ "video moments") to the values and concepts we want them to live by.

Experiential Recognition is my term for the second technique, where we use positive reflections to help instill values. We create, for the child, a picture of a current or recent event, and we frame it in a way that shows the child how a desirable value is or was reflected in that moment. You can help your children recognize when their natural behaviors are reflective of the values you wish them to hold.

Let's use some of the same examples we used for Active Recognition, adding the element of values education:

"I see that you are using red, yellow and green yarn to make your weaving. You are sticking with it, even though it's taking several class periods to finish. Great work! Great perseverance."

"I can hear that you and your other group members are collaborating on your homework project. You're being a valuable member of the team, showing cooperation. I appreciate that."

"I see that you're really frustrated right now. And you're handling those tough feelings without lashing out or yelling at anyone. You are using great restraint and power and using good judgment."

What Are Values?

Values are qualities of behavior, thought and character regarded by a society as intrinsically good; as having desirable results; and that are worthy of imitation by others. They are the principles that govern behavior and reflect what is considered to be good or bad, or moral and immoral, in a culture. In essence they are attributes of the heart.

Think for a moment about the values you want to teach your children. Your list might include some or all of the following:

Peace	Humility
Patience	Fairness
Respect	Responsibility
Friendship	Wisdom
Tolerance	Freedom of expression
Integrity	Good judgment
Helpfulness	Cooperation
Leadership	Using good manners
Perseverance	Compassion
Confidence	Thoughtfulness
Courage	Consideration
Kindness	Open-mindedness
Honesty	Good sportsmanship
Self-control	Doing one's best

The three-page list in the previous chapter includes many other values around which you can create greatness and inner wealth for your children.

We can talk and talk about these values to our children without really teaching them how to *live* those values. We have far greater impact when we teach values *experientially* – in a way that is relevant and an outgrowth of the child's actual life; and in a way that holds the mirror up to the child while he is in the very act of exhibiting the values we wish to teach.

One Head Start teacher who was using the Nurtured Heart Approach told me this story. Her school mandated that she gather her four- and five-year-old students together for "rug time" between activities. Before implementing the approach, it had been like herding cats – a few children would sit down, and by the time she got the others down, the first few were up again. Then, at the start of rug time, she began to teach words like "integrity" and "responsibility" in the context of pointing out each child's greatness: "Alex, I saw you using integrity on the playground. You could have kept on riding your bike when Cathy fell, but you stopped and took care of her and then got an adult over. You were being caring and responsible. Thanks for showing integrity." Since this teacher implemented Experiential Recognitions, her students can't wait for rug time – and they even began to offer up their own additions to the recognitions offered by the teacher! The children actually began to applaud one another after each appreciation; the teacher continued to introduce new, interesting words pertaining to values in the context of the children's experiences.

Think about the typical "teaching moment" in your household. If you're like most parents, you lecture your children in great detail about the values they are *not* reflecting in their behavior. In the midst of emerging problems, our urge to teach what we deem to be "the important lessons of life" fires up in an automatic way.

"Hannah, that's NOT very considerate!" you holler when Hannah swipes the crayons from her sister. As you launch into your lecture about waiting your turn and thinking of others' feelings, Hannah's on the defensive. She's probably not going to walk away from this interaction with an internal desire to be more considerate.

How receptive are *you* to self-improvement when you're being told how you fall short? Why should we expect our children to be receptive when they're feeling confused? Remember, they're getting those energetic $100 bills tossed at them, receiving your focus and energized response around something negative. The child may have confusing, conflicted feelings of enjoying the focus and energy from her favorite "toy" while simultaneously feeling upset by the anger and criticism she's experiencing.

No matter how eloquent you might be, a child who's being lectured about values when she's feeling angry or bad about herself is not going to get the substance of your lecture. She'll just get the confusing energetic message of having your full attention and connection as a direct consequence of having done something she wasn't supposed to do.

Energetically, we are rewarding her misbehavior. If you water weeds, the weeds will grow. And as any gardener knows, weeds don't need a lot of encouragement.

When applying this technique:

- **Start with an Active Recognition and add a comment about how what the child is doing or has done is a reflection of a value you wish to instill.** "Freeze-frame" a picture of success in the here and now. Give clear, specific feedback on values, behaviors or attitudes you consider desirable. You're giving the child an easily "digestible" moment of success, framing a lesson about values in the context of the child's experience.

  "I see that you are upset, Seth, because you can't go to the movie with your friend. I love that you are being honest by feeling your feelings *and* being cooperative by not taking your anger out on anybody."

  "Jenny, Lisa and Tiffany, you are all playing so well together. You are being wonderful by showing respect and consideration for one another."

- **Make an effort to apply this technique in moments when your child is behaving well.** In moments where your children are behaving well on their own, it's so tempting to tiptoe off and scramble to get as much done as you possibly can. Of course, you should take advantage of quiet moments – but first, and periodically as long as the good behavior lasts, be sure to offer Experiential Recognitions as often as you can.

- **Express your excitement about what you're seeing in the child.** Energize your reflections with lots of vocal variation and volume when you're giving recognition. If there are other children around, they'll catch the fever all the more quickly as they see your response to one child's good choices. Think *short, specific, energized* and *positive.* Be creative. Have fun with it!

- **Remember Shamu; remember the toll-taker's attitude; remember the pencil sharpener.** In other words, remember that every desirable quality has many facets, nuances and manifestations. A positive quality like respect or a good attitude can be reflected and recognized from many angles, each of which you can view as an opportunity to guide and nurture. An abundance of Experiential Recognition opportunities exists to teach the very lessons you may have been dying to teach when things are going wrong. You can dissect the behavior of even the most poorly behaved child on his worst day…and find something to get excited about! Capitalize on the spaces between the moments of mayhem and reflect the truth of those moments.

If you have a particular inclination for a value such as respect or responsibility, realize that such qualities have infinite angles and aspects that can be appreciated and reflected as successes.

You can use Experiential Recognition to help children's study skills, too. Think of the many skills required for academic success: the ability to induce, deduce, summarize, organize, think ahead, plan and apply prior learning to new situations. You can point out how your child is already being successful by applying those valuable skills.

Examples: Experiential Recognition
"I see that you are very focused and using a lot of concentration. That is super effort!"

"Samuel, I heard you ask Alex to stop chasing you, and I see that you got really frustrated when he didn't listen. I like that you used your words first, and then that you chose to walk away. You kept your cool and didn't lash out at him. You used really good judgment and great inner strength."

"James, you're showing a respectful attitude in the soccer game. Excellent sportsmanship."

Building Greatness with Experiential Recognition

Experiential Recognitions deepen children's growing sense of who they are as people of greatness – as having and honing the qualities that comprise a great human being. Experiential Recognitions are really perfect for introducing and recognizing specific and crucial aspects of greatness, including choices that exemplify great values. Those choices set the stage for a great life and for being an excellent example for others. Think of the truly great people you know: Don't they all "walk their talk" and live their values? With this technique, you show your child how to do the same.

For an extra boost, supplement your Experiential Recognitions with an additional statement about how the quality you are recognizing is one of greatness. Metaphorically, you've sent an e-mail honoring the child for living the value, embedded into a first-hand experience, and then you write, "See attachment." That attachment then lets the child know that you consider that very quality to be one of greatness. Point out how the child is living that quality of greatness in this present situation.

For example: "Gabi, I am grateful that you have been so earnest in your intention to do your project well. You could have given up because the demands were so high. You really persevered and had an attitude of integrity and enthusiasm, and these are all qualities of greatness."

"Selah, I want to praise you for the honesty you showed in this tough situation with your friends and family. That is not easy, and doing the right thing like this is a great quality."

"Michael, I appreciate that you wanted to give money to that homeless man. That was great thoughtfulness and compassion."

"Lauren, I really appreciate the great judgment you used in choosing to not hurt your sister's feelings when she was feeling so sensitive. You were very supportive. Making a decision like that is a quality of greatness."

Proactive Recognition

Celebrate Children For Not Breaking Rules:

This third technique builds on both Active and Experiential Recognitions. In this technique, we celebrate and pursue success in moments where a problem is *not* occurring, or when it typically would occur.

Proactive Recognition starts with you, the parent, reexamining the rules of your household. Remember that we need to state rules in a *negative* and *precise* way to make them effective; some adjustment of your rules may prove helpful.

Although rule-breaking is generally seen as something to be avoided, in this approach, we almost *give permission* to the child to go ahead and break the rules. In effect, we're saying: *"It's always been your choice anyway, and I appreciate when you choose not to break a rule; however, if you do break a rule, you just need to know that you get a consequence. After that, you're right back in the game. I don't take it as a personal affront. It's part of your exploration. However, when you are not breaking rules, I am so much more grateful about that great decision. You get the credit!"* This drains all the emotional energy and focus away from the negatives and firmly cements it in the positive.

Just as in sports, a rule violation is always a possibility. Rules are almost always violated by choice rather than by accident. **Seeing rule-breaking as a matter of choice rather than a mistake helps us further appreciate the child's choice not to break the rules.** It heightens our vantage point to view this choice as a function of skill and wisdom; it also helps us as parents to avoid taking rules not broken for granted.

Does Positively Reinforcing the Lack of Poor Choices Drive Kids to Make Those Poor Choices?

Some parents and teachers in my workshops have stated that they don't want to proactively reinforce the choice *not* to break a rule, thinking that "all I'll be doing is giving the kids ideas about how to break rules!" Their fear is that a positive statement like "Thank you for not hitting your sister...you are being considerate in making that choice," would set the stage for exactly that undesirable thing to occur.

At first, this does seem likely, but that's only because we're used to normal upside-down ways of parenting.

If we weren't strongly focusing on successes and devoting little energy to poor choices, this might well be the case. However, with the elements of time-in, deepening inner wealth through supportive recognitions, and the lack of energy toward poor choices, you won't be "giving ideas" about how to break rules. When the child consistently gets reinforced for *not* making the poor choice (like hitting her sister), she goes for the gold.

And you can build inner wealth even further by noticing and reflecting moments where the child may have had the impulse to break a rule just after your acknowledgement of that rule not being broken – but didn't. More success! The impulse to break a rule is okay; breaking the rule is not.

Here is a fact that supports the effectiveness of this technique: I've had tremendous success using it with actual fire setters and other kids with highly problematic behaviors. Once their parents and teachers learned how to appreciate these children for choosing not to set fires and applauded these children's success at managing their impulses, the behaviors evaporated. That's victory – and as the sense of victory deepens, we now have a great child in our midst.

About Strictness

Strictness isn't about being punitive or mean; it's about a thick and clear dividing line between a followed rule and a broken rule. Think about the Ten Commandments. It wasn't "Thou shalt treat others with respect and gentleness," it was "Thou shalt not kill." There isn't much wiggle room there. And wiggle room is the last thing children need when it comes to rules.

This runs contrary to the "positive discipline" approach that is so popular nowadays. But when you read on, you'll find that stating rules in this fashion will give you enormous room for finding success. Vague statements of rules blur the line between success and poor choices, giving you a lot less room to create success and a lot more possibility of leaks of energy and relationship when the child is dancing near, on, or over the line. The beauty of a well- defined line is that it provides clear evidence of when a child has rerouted and chosen NOT to break a rule. The child no longer gets lost in the gray area of fuzzy rules, *and her choices to follow the rules no longer get taken for granted.*

Reconstructing Your House Rules

First, make a written list of your house rules. You may have some that are specific and negative ("no jumping on the furniture" or "no hitting") and some that are general and positive ("be respect-ful" or "do as you're told by a parent"). Then, modify them so that they are all stated negatively and precisely. You may need to break it down and create several rules from the single positively stated rule with which you started out. Let your needs for your house-hold guide you; rules differ in different households, and that's O.K.

EXAMPLES: Old Rules	EXAMPLES: New Rules
Keep your hands to yourself.	No hitting; no pushing; no grabbing things away from others.
Be respectful.	No disrespect; no talking back to adults; no name-calling; no teasing.
Follow directions.	No disobeying a request from a parent.
Use good table manners.	No bad manners; no chewing with your mouth open; no playing with your food; no saying "Eeeew!" when a plate of lovingly prepared, nutritious food is placed before you.

This is where the "strictness" leg of the three-legged table becomes straight and strong. Here are other ideas for rules:

No bad words

No breaking things

No interrupting

No teasing

No arguing

No tantrums

The more rules you have, the more room you'll have to find successes when those rules are *not being broken!* Children rankle against rules because they only ever hear about them when they've broken one and are in trouble for it; but when they see that they can expect positive recognition for *not* breaking rules, they'll see that more rules are actually better...that rules are beneficial.

Rather than making the mistake of simply applauding adherence to rules the child has often broken, **create an entire range of rules that represent a child as a whole person.** If your child never argues or uses bad words or calls others names, aren't these still rules that you expect your child to follow? Plus, this is a perfect opportunity to create rules that you know will be followed, offering ample opportunity to provide positive recognition. Use a full range of rules to push examples of the child's own thoughtfulness and success into the light.

Rules that start with "no" lend themselves to so much more clarity than do "positive" rules. In my observation of many classrooms that attempt to set limits with rules like "Be respectful" and "Act responsibly," the line of demarcation that allows the teacher to say "oops, that's a broken rule" is downright fuzzy. How much disrespect needs to occur before the rule is officially violated? Or how much irresponsibility? This gray area is the place where parents and teachers get sucked into long lectures and warnings as they try to define what is or isn't a broken rule.

If your rules are not clear, you end up giving warning after warning as the child pushes at the boundary. This is a reward for the intense child. Positively stated rules plus unclear consequences are a surefire recipe for escalating patterns of testing by children. They're searching for the boundary, trying to find out how far they have to go to be "out of bounds" and get that negative energetic hit they've grown accustomed (even addicted) to. Parent and child wind up entangled in arguments about where the boundaries are between a rule followed and a rule broken. Proactive Recognitions combined with clear rules circumvent this problem.

As you consistently express your appreciation of rules not broken, you soon will see that your child knows the rules. The child will know for sure that *you* know the rules. At that point, you'll find yourself in a much more advantageous position to *enforce* those rules. You'll wonder how you ever thought you could set limits that didn't exist!

With a challenging child, positive rules actually encourage larger-scale acting out, because mild acting-out can fall between the cracks and go undetected. Wiggly limits cause the child to conclude that blatant transgressions are necessary to make sure they're falling well beyond that ever-moving boundary. And that's what they need to do to feed themselves with the guaranteed energy, relationship and intimacy that rule violations can so readily inspire.

To grow inner wealth and inspire successful choices in the difficult child, we need to show him that the line between rule followed and rule broken is whisper-thin but incredibly strong; that stepping over it will no longer get him the energetic hit he expects; and that adult energy is available only in response to his choice to stay on the right side of that line.

This very same strategy has proven to help the normal child flourish. When you try this with your child, you will quickly see that you are talking a language your children can really hear. They will "get" that you "get them."

The Time-Out: A Brief Introduction
The time-out is nothing but a brief disengagement from interaction and positive recognitions. The child soon sees that it's nothing to be feared. She won't feel the need to argue her way out of it. **The time-out is not so much a "punishment" as a reset** – a moment where the child is instructed to "chill" and pause. (Again, if you need more on this now, refer to Chapter 6.)

There's absolutely no engagement about the broken rule until the time-out is over. Then, you and your child get right back "into the game" (of building successes), and you can immediately create a success through which you teach the rule in question: "Thanks so much for sitting through that time-out, Judy. Now you aren't teasing your sister...you're demonstrating respect. That is a great quality."

This absence of your interaction and energy in any form becomes a true consequence, but it is only momentary, a brief time-out. Under this approach, a true consequence becomes a wonderful vehicle for teaching the very same lessons you've been dying to teach, except that now you are giving it this abidingly positive slant.

So many parents I've met were desperately trying to play "hardball" when things went awry; and to their dismay, they found that escalating consequences continued to backfire. This is an alternate way of playing hardball: First, play hardball with successes and with refusing to energize negativity; then, play hardball with consequences by never looking the other way when a rule is broken.

Challenging children in particular require extremely precise rules – clear demarcations between right and wrong. All children thrive when the line between "in bounds" and "out of bounds" is clear and precise. Without that, you end up with all kinds of border skirmishes and disagreements over whether a rule has been broken or not, warnings, and ultimately more energy and relationship accidentally rewarding the act of pushing the limits. You yourself may even struggle to figure out whether Joey was really following directions or not or whether Amanda was really being disrespectful.

You require clarity, too, in order to zoom in and make observations about the child's successes in following the rules you have established. The referee in sports needs the clarity of the line to truly know whether the foot is on or over the line. Without the clarity, there is a breeding ground for potential chaos.

When applying this technique:

- **Take a moment where your child is following the rules, view it as a photo opportunity, and then celebrate it verbally.** With this technique, you can "hijack" children into a deeper realm of success – a vital aspect of his newly emerging portfolio.

Soon, the child no longer only feels seen when breaking rules and invisible when he's not. And now he is being recognized for far more than behaving – he's being recognized for *making wise decisions*, and that's going to expand his inner wealth tremendously. Being told that you "know how to behave" has far less impact than being told that you are appreciated for using the wisdom to make good choices. It's a new realm of power and capability in relation to the rules. It helps a child feel that he can not only manage his life, but that he can do it with greatness!

Even the most challenging child can't help but follow the rules some of the time, especially if you have included rules that you know are "a given" for your child. This strategy will greatly enhance the child's sense of opportunity and accomplishment.

- **Consciously find moments when nothing seems to be happening; then, capture those moments by acknowledging your child for not breaking the rules or pushing the limits in that given instant.**

Be on the lookout for gradations and nuances of rule adherence to help move that rope up and up beneath the water. Let's say that you've called the whole clan to breakfast. Peter might be horsing around or going really slowly in an effort to evoke an energized reaction from you. As long as he is moving in a positive direction and not breaking any rules, find the good in what he's doing: "Peter, I see that you're starting to move toward your chair. You're making a good choice. I appreciate that you are not disobeying my directions." Or, you can ignore his testing behavior (as long as no rule is being broken) and give your praise to your other children who are already seated. Always work to most highly energize those showing the highest standards. Just one caution: Be careful not to do this in a way that is shaming to the child.

- **Create at least one rule – preferably many – that your child seldom (if ever) breaks.** This gives you ammunition for Experiential Recognition no matter what happens to be hitting the fan at any given time.
- **Tell the truth of this moment and leave the past and future out of it.** The child may have argued three minutes ago, and may be about to argue again, but right now, she isn't. Energize this moment, and this moment, and this moment. Staying with the truth of the moment will give you much more opportunity to bring forth success and to influence the transformative change you are seeking. And staying in your heart will allow you to experience authentic appreciation and gratitude. For example, if you have a child who is aggressive at times, worry, fear and shame can easily be overwhelming. But if you allow yourself to experience gratitude in your heart when aggression *isn't* happening, and you share that gratitude with your child, you are giving words to your heart's song.
- **Don't concern yourself, at the outset, with having a big discussion of "the new rules" with your children.** Think of the video game concept. Children do not get a new video game and dive into the rulebook before playing. They load that game up and learn as they go. That's the bulk of the fun! Most players don't know all the rules going in; they learn them as a result of seeing what happens when rules are broken and when they are not. And then they're right back in there, exercising their new understanding of the game's rules.

Although some parents choose to post their rules, you don't have to do that either. Posting alone is no guarantee that rules will be learned and abided by. Children best learn them experientially through your targeting and appreciating their successful "non-breaking" of those rules and through your delivery of short, un-energized consequences when they *are* broken.

You, however, need to know all of your rules cold. This will enable you to have the clarity to employ positive recognition when rules are not being broken and to give a brief time-out when a rule is broken. "Oops! Broke a rule," you'll say. At first, the child might protest that he *didn't* break a rule or that he didn't know there was such a rule. Don't go there; let the time-out finish first (starting when the child stops arguing his point), and then frame that rule in terms of the child now following it successfully.

That reframe to success alone will establish the presence of the newly minted rule. No other discussion is needed. One thing you can trust is that the vast majority of times a rule is broken, the child knows it, even if it was never formally spelled out.

Let this form of reset be extremely brief. Simply and silently turn away if necessary. Even a few seconds serves the purpose of having your child perceive a result of his actions; then move to the next new moment of success – which is the ultimate purpose of the reset.

• **Let the child be taught the rules through the experience of following them and being acknowledged for that.** Make her feel thoughtful and wise; she will take it from there.

Proactive Recognition: Examples

"Brandon, I appreciate that you have not used foul language at all this morning. Thanks for following the rules."

"Jason, I like that you are not teasing your brother. That's a good example of following the rules and also a great way to be a friend."

"Susan, I notice that you have stayed focused on homework for quite a while now without getting distracted. Thank you for obeying the rule that homework time is only for doing homework."

"Jon, I love that you haven't argued with me at all while I've been helping you finish your project. That shows you are patient."

"Maria, I want you to know how much I appreciate that you are being so gentle with the cat. You are not doing anything that would hurt or bother her. You are showing you can really be trusted with the feelings of others."

"Franklin, you're using your power to handle your strong feelings, and you aren't being aggressive or breaking anything even though you are really sad and upset. That is true strength."

At the instant Josh *finally* pipes down for a second after being incredibly fidgety during a family meal: "Josh, I see that you are sitting quietly in your seat and eating and not getting distracted. Thanks for following the rules about meal times."

As trouble brews between two siblings, find a way to head off the physical violence by acknowledging the successes going on: "Ian, I'm seeing that you are very angry with your brother right now, but you're using your self-control and not getting rough with him. You're showing patience and compassion."

In the last example, a bit of explanation might be helpful. It's not a crime to be mad at someone; the choice is to celebrate his effective ways of handling that anger. If it's contained and handled well, there's reason to celebrate – because the fact is it could have been handled poorly.

Be discerning and tell the truth of the moment. If the child crosses the line in the next instant, give the consequence, and when things are back to being handled well, give the compliment.

How Much Praise Is Too Much?

You can't praise too much – as long as it's coming from your genuine observations of the child's successes.

I have, like everyone else, experienced compliments that felt like blowing smoke – praise that lacks substance or sincerity. When you stick to the truth of the moment and the authenticity of your heart, however, this will never be the case.

Building Greatness with Proactive Recognition

Proactive Recognitions wonderfully advance the overarching intention of building resounding inner wealth and guiding your child to an inner sense of greatness.

Deciding to follow the rules despite their sometimes confining nature is a sign of emerging wisdom and power. It represents collaboration, capability and discernment – all qualities that you naturally want to promote. Why not water those seeds of greatness? Wouldn't you agree that these are truly qualities of a great person? Wouldn't you love to see these great qualities emerge in ever more expansive ways? Wouldn't

you love to see these qualities become more solid and endur-
ing in your child?

One counselor wrote to me about her experience using this
approach with adult methamphetamine addicts. She has had
dramatic results with individuals whom others in her field
had declared impervious to treatment. She often "accuses"
these addicts of success. The intensity of this recognition of
successes is enough, in many cases, to shake these addicts
into a new perception of themselves: as great mothers, as
great workers, as simply great. And this is what's needed to
move them away from their addictions.

In essence, we are confronting a person's previous reality
with our perception of a new reality. We are saying, "It's not
a question of whether you can or can't be great. Here you are
right now *being* great. Here's how you are doing that, and I
see it right now in my lens…and I need to tell you."

For example:

"Maggie, choosing not to grab back that toy from your brother
shows me that you really think about things before you decide
what to do. You chose to be considerate, and you chose to not
break the rule. Choosing to be fair is a great quality that you
have."

"I notice that you made a very big decision, Ben, to go to the
family event without arguing or fussing. I can tell you really
didn't want to go, and in the past you might have gone bal-
listic. You are showing qualities I consider to be great: wisdom and healthy power. A lot of kids think power has to do
with aggression, but great power has to do with great decisions and great actions."

"Allie, I very much appreciate that you went the extra mile to
complete your homework tonight. I know it's late, you are
tired, it's been a long day, and the assignment was way too
much. You could have thrown a fit or even used bad words,

but you didn't. That really shows me your great inner strength and perseverance and great capability. Thanks for living in your greatness. It's not always easy."

These examples might seem a little wordy and long-winded – although **most of us probably could wax at least this poetically if something were going *wrong* without batting an eyelash. The challenge is to give "the lecture" when things are going right.** This is when all the desired lessons will have the greatest impact and when your child will be most receptive.

Creative Recognition

Hijacking Children into Success:

This technique creates situations that will transport even especially challenging children into success while promoting any child's sense of cooperation and collaboration. I call it Creative Recognition because you are using your creativity to "hijack" your child further into success by *creating successes that would otherwise not happen.* We *steal* these opportunities – but it's a good form of larceny, rest assured!

Every day, we expect our children to do specific things, like brush their teeth, get ready for school, put their things away, behave well in school and do their homework. The average child may easily follow directions to do these things, and some children are great at scheduling and regulating themselves to do all they're expected to do.

In contrast, more intense or challenging children – the ones who often seem to be causing disruptions and problems – will perceive a request as an easy opportunity to extract energy and relationship from you *by not complying.*

Imagine the child who is asked pleasantly, "Would you please set the table?" You can almost hear this child's hard drive ticking as he evaluates the options on the desktop of his mind. There, he has folders containing ever-accumulating evidence of what is true.

One folder is labeled "When I Comply" and it's full of skimpy, low-energy parental responses, little shreds of mild positivity like "thank you" and "good job." Another folder, labeled "When I Don't Comply," is packed with examples of heightened relationship and excitement because the child is accustomed to a big blast of intimacy and energy every time he refuses to do your bidding. Which folder do you think he'll open up?

In this category of recognition, we essentially *create* the compliance before the child can do otherwise...and then we demonstrate that he gets that energetic hit, the intimate connection and the heightened level of presence for the successful choice. We fill up that "When I Comply" folder with evidence that there is abundant energy and relationship for success and for following the rules.

When applying this technique:

- Start with an utterly doable request. Make the request, then energize the child's response and effort. Make failure impossible and then make a BIG deal when the child does as you ask. Hold on to the Shamu and toll-taker concepts – creating successes that would not otherwise exist and choosing to see the positive side of things – just as in the previous techniques.

  Let's say that your child is getting into the car and buckling up. As soon as you see the child starting to do this, say, "I need you to buckle up." She's already started the action but you are taking advantage of it for the purpose of creating success related to requests. Then remark how cooperative she is for having made that good choice to follow your instructions.

- Avoid polite or diplomatic ways of starting out a request, like "Would you…" or "Could you…" or "Please…." Here's an important point about telling your children to do whatever it is you need them to do: Do not *ask* them. "Would you please…?" "Could you…?" "Would you mind…?" Obviously, these ways of requesting a child to do something imply a choice and open the door for the child to say "No" or refuse by way of non-action. Don't provide this opportunity in any shape or form. Clearly state your request as "I need you to…" or "I want you to…" or "Go ahead and…."

  "I don't think it's a good idea for you to go outside without your jacket" leaves room for your child to protest your idea. Instead, say: "I need you to put on your jacket." Instead of "Why aren't you able to sit in your seat like everyone else does?" try "I want you to sit in your seat."

  Let's say you want your child to get in the car and buckle up. Don't *ask* or say please, both of which imply a choice. And by all means, don't say: "You still haven't…" when she goofs around and does everything *but* what you've asked. If she doesn't sit and buckle up when told to, a rule is being broken, and a time-out/reset is in order. Of course, once the time-out is completed and the child is appreciated for doing her consequence well, then the original request is still in effect. "Now I need you to get your seat belt fastened."

- **Convey a message that every movement in the right direction is valued.** Here, we put the pencil sharpener notion into action. Cultivate a *microscopic view* of the child's successful behaviors. Find and praise at first even the smallest successes or steps toward success. Increase the child's awareness of small steps, choices and behaviors that are desirable or laudable. **Keep in mind always that a child isn't going to want to run a race he thinks he can't win.** Show him how he's already making a winning step and he'll begin wanting to get in there and run.

- **When resistance comes up, remember your stands: relentless pursuit of positivity; strict rule enforcement; and no leaks of negativity.** It's fairly common, at first, for children to resist, test and try to either brush off your praise or actively pull you back into the negative patterns they have grown comfortable with. If you're being tested, return to the three-legged table. Use it like a mantra. Tell yourself: "I won't let my children pull me into a pattern of failure and payoffs for negativity. I will do what it takes to pull them in the direction of success." Don't back off on the positives when they resist; if anything, turn up the dial!

  Creative Recognition is great for all of your children but is a particularly powerful tool for the more challenging child, where it can be used to create rich experiences of success and inner wealth where most needed. Used in this way, Creative Recognition will transform the former pattern of procrastination and defiance to one of collaboration and success and add to the overall progression of inner wealth.

Creative Recognition: Examples

At clean-up time, a request is made: "I need you to get started" and the child pushes blocks slowly but in the general direction of the block bin: "I notice that you're starting to put the blocks in the bin. I really appreciate how well you listened when I said it was time to clean up."

You've told the kids that it's time to start preparing for bed. Just as the child looks up from his computer or the TV and starts to stretch and get up – maybe not with the intention of heading to his room to change into pajamas – try: "I see you getting ready to go and put on your PJs. I appreciate that you're getting up and are starting to do as I asked. You're following direction and I like that!"

You're at the front door of your home with a bag of groceries. "Here, hold this for a second," you tell your child, handing her the bag while you dig out your keys and unlock the door. "Thanks so much for being so attentive and grabbing that bag for me when I asked you to. You did it with such a helpful, cooperative attitude."

You can even give a child a directive *while he is in the act*. For example, say "Put your dirty clothes in the hamper" to a child who is already doing so. Then praise him for one or more of the following, or anything else you're heart directs you to say at the moment: his collaborative attitude, his forethought, his amazing anticipation, his quick estimation of what needed to happen, or his great example to others.

With the Shamu and toll-taker stories in mind, you can "steal" even more opportunity. Making requests with which the child is highly likely to comply will promote greater levels of independence and responsibility in the weeks and months to come.

Joseph's Story

In my clinical practice some time ago, I started a series of therapy sessions with a family with a child named Joseph. This child was pretty much off the map in terms of compliance – six years old and as oppositional as they come.

Does anyone doubt that a six-year-old can single-handedly unravel a school? Actually, Joseph attended a fairly savvy school that had worked well with challenging children of lesser intensity and determination. Joseph, however, had an uncanny knack for getting himself tossed out of class on any day he pleased. Once he had done so, he would be escorted to the office (*Reward! Relationship!*) where he typically threw himself on the floor like a wet noodle.

At that point he had a bevy of administrators and office personnel at his fingertips. He was, energetically at least, treated like royalty. No matter what was said at that point in time, the battle was lost; the adults clearly were rewarding Joseph's poor choices with abundant relationship and response.

The school wasn't asking for help; Joseph's parents were. I explained the concepts of the Nurtured Heart Approach to these beleaguered parents, and more than 10 years later I still remember Joseph's father's response with complete clarity. He looked at me as though I were a total fool and said, "You don't get it, do you? Joseph has never done anything we've asked him to do, and frankly, I don't believe he's going to start cooperating any time soon."

This put me on alert as to the severity of the situation. I cranked up my explanations, trying to clarify the "larcenous" aspect of the approach. I said, "I hear your concern, so I'll tell you in advance that the way to go is to make these requests in a way that causes him to literally trip over opportunities to succeed. Be as tricky as you need to be."

The father rolled his eyes as if to say, "*No chance,*" and soon the session ended and the family left. But the next time I saw them, the father smiled a wry little smile, and I asked, "So, how'd you do it?" He replied: "Joseph was getting into the car; he sat down and was pulling the door closed. Then I asked him to close the door. It was already half done; it was too late to reverse it!" When that door clicked closed, the father said, "Joseph, thanks for doing just what I asked you to do. That's great following directions."

Now *that's* a home run. I asked what came next, and it turned out to be a *grand slam* home run: Joseph clicked his seatbelt on, and his dad turned around and *told him to put his seatbelt on.* And again, his father "accused" him of being successful. Brilliant! It was a done deal. He said to his son, "Wow! This time, it was almost as if you heard my request inside your brain and I didn't even have to say it! You knew what I wanted and you cooperated. I appreciate that."

To make a long story short, the unimaginable transpired: Within a few weeks, you could ask Joseph to clean his room or do his homework – and *he would simply do it.* The parents had to start somewhere, and they made the Shamu and toll-taker concepts work beautifully for themselves in their quest to help their child move into a more positive space.

Existence = Success

Here's another take on Creative Recognition: You can creatively recognize your child by linking the child's very existence to something great and wonderful.

"It's such fun to have you in this family."

"Your presence adds a needed calmness to the family."

"I like seeing how your siblings smile when you enter the room."

"I love the energy and enthusiasm that you bring to all you do."

As with the previous recognitions, Creative Recognition is meant to work in the moment. Telling the truth of this moment and leaving the past and future out of it opens a doorway to a spiritual level of interaction and awareness. Time slows down; truth is laid bare. In my experience, when one is celebrating the "yes" of this moment, it feels as though God or Spirit joins forces, multiplying greatness.

The child may have argued three minutes ago, and may be about to argue again, but right now, she isn't. **That's all the lens of the camera can ever really digest: the flash of this instant.** Maybe that's why so many people are fascinated with the magic of photography – because it captures a moment, unfailingly bringing one into the now. The most compelling photographs often are those that are the least posed. They are true reflections of the now. Postured successes don't hold a candle to the utter and compelling simplicity of human moments.

Energize this moment, and this moment, and this moment. Reflect back to your children the greatness you see that they would otherwise miss. Shine the dazzling light of success back into their eyes; that light will come to shine ever more brightly. Celebrate!

Making a Big Deal

Every now and then, I meet someone who tells me they're quite nervous about the notion of making a big deal over his or her child's successes. "I see how pivotal this piece is to helping my child...but when it comes time to actually use the Nurtured Heart language, and do it with energy and enthusiasm, I just feel like I can't do it. Nothing comes out."

Some will go on to explain that, in their own upbringings, the adults rarely had anything good to say; in stark contrast, mountains were often made of all the negative molehills. And although most of these parents claimed to dislike having grown up in this environment, they also couldn't seem to break the pattern after becoming parents themselves.

I have good news for people with this concern. I tell them that they probably don't need to go through years of therapy to combat this type of history. My experience is, in fact, that this kind of history provides them with an *advantage*. They know what a big deal feels like. They know what it's like to get worked up and emotional about even the smallest things; to go over the top.

I tell them: "Keep making a big deal – but make it over successes."

Building Greatness with Creative Recognition

Creative Recognitions help you purposefully hone crucial qualities of greatness such as helpfulness, consideration, cooperation, participation and collaboration.

This strategy enables the parent to bring out the best in the child, sending creative messages that express pure enjoyment of the child's existence, and the meaning that has for the parent.

For example:

"David, thanks so much for following my directions. That shows great consideration and collaboration. You listened to what I asked, and took care of it. You are really participating in the needs of this family and that is a great quality."

"Danielle, your intelligent and spirited solutions show me how much you care about our well-being. You are always making such great contributions."

"Christopher, I want to tell you something important. When you collaborated just now to help set up for dinner, you not only did it efficiently but you did it with a wonderful and pleasant attitude. That is a great quality that I admire in you. Thanks so much."

"Lisa, you bring such great inspiration to our work together. It means so much to me and I value that so much. What a great contribution you make by letting your inspiration flow."

Can compliments of this caliber actually register with kids? The answer is *yes,* and you will see the difference this makes in their lives. Your comments bring your child to feel great about himself. As he assimilates those reflections in ever-deeper ways, you'll see a shift as he realizes: "Yes, that IS me!" From that point onward, you will see more and more spontaneous manifestations of greatness that will warm your heart. Promise.

Putting It All Together to Build Inner Wealth in Your Children

All these techniques build on one another and are designed to be used fluidly, in combination. Start with the first, the "Video Moments," and build to Experiential Recognition (teaching values), then Proactive Recognition (teaching rules), and finally, Creative Recognition. Practice your vocabulary to where you can shower your children with praise effortlessly.

Once you've gotten through the initial learning curve, and once it stops feeling counterintuitive, you'll find that it takes between five and ten seconds to give a positive recognition. If you went really rapid-fire with it, you could do 50 of these recognitions in five minutes. Not that you would, but if you had to, and you were feeling especially jazzed and creative, you could. Spread out across the total amount of time you spend with your child each day, does it seem unreasonable to think you could give 10, 20 or 30 positive recognitions in a day? **That's far less than five minutes of your total day.**

More difficult, intense or withdrawn children will likely require a more aggressive, time-intensive application than children who are within the realm of "normal" and who have, in the past, responded at least partially to traditional disciplinary and parenting approaches.

The quality of the approach will be the same no matter what; it's only the intensity of the application that will vary from child to child. And you can't "overuse" the approach; if you have one challenging child and one not-so-challenging child, you can apply the techniques equally to the benefit of both. (Really, you *should* apply the techniques equally, because the less challenging child won't tolerate getting the short end of the stick for long.)

The simplicity and brevity of this approach are a key reason it is so effective. It cuts to the heart of information that most strongly motivates and encourages children. If your praises or requests get too vague or confusing, you may end up sending the wrong message. Keep working to make what the child can value in his or her self abundantly clear.

With the right camera angles and intention, it's not hard at all to communicate successes back to even the most challenging child. And, better yet, my experience overwhelmingly has been that doing so quickly transports children to a wonderful and fruitful new portfolio of **who they really are.** They have a first-hand experience of their greatness and divine nature.

CHAPTER SIX

The New Time-Out

Stand I is the *relentless pursuit of positivity* and Stand III the *refusal to leak negativity*. If those are two legs of our three-legged table, we still need another one to get it standing, and that's Stand II: *strict rule enforcement*. And that brings us to the joint topics of *limit-setting* and *consequences*.

This chapter will provide you with a reliable, consistent frame of reference for understanding and implementing consequences. If you play your hand well, consequences end up generating even more success.

Giving Permission to Break Rules

Adults and children have come to see rule-breaking as a terrible thing that must be avoided at all costs. Warnings, lectures and other kinds of intense connection often surface around trying to *prevent* children from breaking rules.

But focusing on trying to *prevent* rule-breaking contributes more energy toward negative behaviors. When adults stop thinking in terms of preventing rule-breaking – when they step aside and allow children to experience *what really happens* when they break a rule – the children have an inescapably clear first-hand experience that helps cement their understanding of the benefits they receive for following them.

Besides: children know perfectly well that if they really *want* to break a rule, there's not much anyone can do to stop them. Admonishments and threats ("Now, Hope, if you eat that candy, that'll be a broken rule!") put more fuel on the fire we're trying to extinguish.

Keep in mind that breaking rules is part of learning the world. Just be sure to refuse to look the other way when a consequence is needed. The child will soon see that the new consequences he faces aren't drastic or punitive. They amount to a simple "reset" before the child can jump back into the game.

Freedom from Escalating Consequences

Typically, when a child chooses to break a rule, parents reflexively "launch their software" – diving in with energized words of wisdom about all the reasons it's not okay to break the rules. With energetically upside-down parenting approaches, no matter what method we choose as a consequence – natural/logical consequences, removing privileges, giving extra chores, administering a long lecture – it's the passion and energy we give those methods that keep inadvertently awarding the child those energetic $100 bills for doing the wrong things.

The purpose of consequences in the Nurtured Heart Approach is to maintain the default to positivity. We don't use warnings or lectures, but a simple, brief and immediate consequence for a rule broken. Think in terms of a consequence for a minor infraction in a sporting event or a quick reset in a video game. The consequence is over quickly and it's right back to the success the game brings by default.

Our culture has come to believe that a consequence has to be drastic in order to work. It has to *hurt,* most believe, or it won't be effective in changing the child's ways. There is some logic to this, and it works to keep most children in line to some extent. But I contend the level of punishment or severity of a consequence is not what makes it powerful. *A longer, stronger, louder or more frightening consequence is not the thing that will awaken the child to the error of his ways and drive him never to do that deed again.*

Here's what brings the child to a place where he does not want to break the rules: an awakening to his successfulness and greatness. Why bother breaking the rules when rule-breaking only gets in the way of the fun of being in the game?

In traditional parenting methods, the time-out usually calls for adding a minute to the time-out for each year of the child's age. A one-year-old sitting still for a minute is a pretty absurd notion; and a three-year-old for three minutes? Good luck! Impracticality aside, this method speaks to the idea that adding minutes will add to the time-out's impact. In my experience, I have not found this to be the case.

The real truth is that *time-out is an illusion*; it's about the child *perceiving* that a result has taken place. The power of the consequence lies in creating a momentary interruption in the occurrence of the problem. And the purpose of the interruption is to *allow the parent to jump to the next available moment of success* – where inner wealth can be further expanded.

Warnings and Lectures Energize Problems

Warnings are leaks of negativity. You're throwing another log on the very fire you are trying to put out. It won't get you where you want to go. Warnings still carry the charge of energy and relationship. Saying to a child, "Joey, I don't like when you are mean to your brother... now don't do that again!" keeps handing out evidence of relationship when things are going wrong, especially for the child who has come to feel relatively invisible when he's not bothering his brother.

The other problem with warnings is that they inhibit consistent rule enforcement. Although in our society we tend to think of warnings as compassionate, the fact is that the **inconsistency caused by warnings creates an unpredictable world for the child.** Really, this is anything *but* compassionate. If a rule is not enforced consistently, it isn't a rule.

Warnings can easily become a moving target. When Mom or Dad is having a great day and everything seems rosy, they might let a few rule infractions slide and give a few extra warnings. On a more frustrating day, the parent may have less patience, giving fewer warnings or none at all before meting out the lectures, anger or punishment.

For the difficult child, lectures, warnings, second chances, and even traditional punishments function as rewards. When the child "gets in trouble," she becomes the center of attention and receives lots of words and relationship from adults who are trying their best to set her straight. Even as she feels like a failure, she's fed by all that energy, whether it's a gentle heart-to-heart or a 30-minute yell-fest. Is it any wonder she goes back for more within hours or minutes?

The child knows, as surely as she's breathing, that adults always seem to have time for problems. A child needful of your time and energy will be drawn to create problems, just as water is drawn down an open drain. Once you learn to be very strict and positive, and to stop pouring your energy into problems, things will turn around fast.

If you have words of wisdom to impart to your child regarding his behavior, wait until the consequence has been delivered and served. Then, watch like a hawk for the child to reflect the choices you were itching to steer him toward and leap in to point out his successes. You can give a lecture, make a big deal or launch your words of wisdom – as long as it's done through the progressive building of your child's inner wealth. It's your timing that matters: As long as your words of wisdom come out when things are not going wrong, your timing is right.

The Clean Time-Out

Most of the consequences commonly used are, in essence, a time-out. They all distill down to the same core: a temporary loss of life's options, energies and relationships. The child's inner feeling is that of being out of the loop.

Under the Nurtured Heart Approach, I recommend using only a **brief, clean time-out** when it's consequence time. By "clean" I mean with absolutely no fanfare – the simplest of instructions given with no energy or emotion. When a rule is broken, even to the slightest degree, say something like:

- "Oops, broke a rule. Time-out."
- "That's a broken rule."
- "Jody, time-out" or "Jody, reset."
- "Red light!" (Use "green light" to return to time-in.)
- "Pause!" (Use "play" to return to time-in.)

In other words, use whatever works for you but keep it simple and straightforward. Parents and teachers get wonderfully creative with their own versions.

Keep time-outs short! They can last anywhere from two seconds to a minute, but no more.

Yes, you read that right: two seconds to a minute. It works as long as the lavishly positive time-in is waiting on the other side.

If time-in is insignificant, this kind of time-out will have no effect whatsoever. If time-in is sufficiently strong, this kind of brief time-out can move mountains.

Back to Time-In

As soon as the child completes the time-out, take immediate advantage of the opportunity to point out more success. For example: "Andy, you sat so well through that time-out. I appreciate that you were able to accept the consequences of breaking a rule, even though you were angry with me for giving the time-out. That's a wonderful decision you made."

Even if you had to struggle to get him there, even if it took him a while to settle down – somehow, some way, he eventually calmed down enough to complete the consequence. That needs to be commended. And that compliment will promote more great choices, cooperation and inner strength in the future.

What if a Child Refuses the Time-Out?

There will be times when a child absolutely refuses to do even the two-second version of the reset, particularly when you first begin to apply the Nurtured Heart Approach. She may dig in stubbornly, going to the mat to try to extract energized connection from you in response to her refusal. How should you handle this situation?

Remember that, from the standpoint of this approach, consequences are essentially an illusion. The truly desired movement in the direction of positive choices happens as a result of the child's ever-blossoming *experiences of being reflected as successful and great.* In this context, a time-out can be a blink of the eye; it can be the child's briefest moment of stillness. Even a movement toward stillness can be recognized and used to guide the child into success: "Great job, Jonah! Your time-out is over, and you did it even though you're feeling angry. I can see you making the effort to control yourself. Excellent judgment."

If you view time-out as consisting simply of the child being temporarily out of a game that's exciting to be part of, the child doesn't actually have to move a muscle or go anywhere. The time-out can be as simple as the adult turning away for a few moments, turning back and declaring it over and successful. It's the words denoting closure that give the child the perception of completion and of having had a result of the broken rule.

This intervention is guided by the principles relayed in the stories of Shamu and the toll-taker: purposely continue, even through a consequence, to move inexorably into more success and greatness.

Time-Out Tips

DON'T escalate or energize when the child doesn't jump into time-out right away.	DO allow the child a few moments to accept and begin the time-out. Nagging or pressuring the child to start the time-out is tantamount to handing out more $100 bills for poor choices.
DON'T thank a child for completing the time-out without saying *why* you are appreciative. Then, rather than conveying that the child is doing you a favor; you are acknowledging that she has made a wise choice.	DO acknowledge the child's self-control and ability to redirect himself; or his maturity in accepting the consequences of his actions; or the good example he's setting for his siblings by quickly accepting his time-out and getting back on track.
DON'T explain which rule has been broken.	DO trust that the child knows which rule has been broken. Keep a sharp eye out for demonstrations of that same rule being followed rather than broken, then reflect that back to the child: "Jenny, I see that you're now choosing to sit peacefully in your chair and eat your dinner instead of teasing your sister. You are following the rules now and showing good focus and respect for others."

DON'T be roped into a battle over whether time-out is needed, or react to any displays of bad attitude that arise in response to the time-out.	DO drain all the energy, relationship, effort, emotion and time from your responses to your child's negative reaction to a time-out. Remain unaffected by pleading, arguing, insults, tantrums and fussing engaged in by the child to try to get your features popping.
DON'T add more time to the time-out in response to the child's resistance or spend time explaining the infraction after the time-out ends.	DO just enforce the original time-out.
DON'T designate a special place or area for time-outs. That just gives the child more ways in which to refuse and cause disruption. Your goal is always to spend as little time and energy on time-out as possible.	DO carry out the consequence exactly where you are when the rule is broken. You can "accuse" the child of completing time-out successfully without his having moved an inch. It's the child's perception of the reset that counts in yielding the result.
DON'T engage in any discussion or explanation of problems, hold grudges, point fingers, blame or give the consequence in a way that's shaming or humiliating.	DO stay in the moment. Keep your cool, no matter what. Be strict, but not stern; use a calm but strong voice. Get the time-out over with and move on to the next moment. Simply deliver the consequence, each and every time a rule is broken, and make a big deal over the child's successful completion of the time-out.
DON'T forget to close the time-out; don't give the child control over ending the time-out.	DO always notify the child when a time-out has been successfully completed.

DON'T allow the child to contribute in any way to whatever's going on while he's in a time-out.	DO remember that the child is "out of the game" (of life) however briefly he is in time-out. Keep time-outs short and demonstrate how energy flows readily and generously as soon as the time-out ends.
DON'T take rule breaking as a personal offense ("How could she keep DOING this to me? Is she TRYING to make me mad?"). And DON'T seek apologies or promises ("Do you PROMISE never to do that AGAIN?").	DO see the time-out as an interruption of the problem – a diversion, not a punitive consequence. Optimally it serves as a perfect lead-in to the next, greater level of new success and a deepening of inner wealth.
DON'T try to mediate the child's problem with others.	DO watch for broken rules and successes, enforce rules and reflect successes; the rest will take care of itself.
DON'T give a time-out in *anticipation* of a rule about to be broken. If a rule hasn't been broken, you can actually still applaud the success of the choice not to break a rule.	DO remember that either a rule has been broken or it hasn't. Expect success. If you expect success, your child will succeed.
DON'T back off on the positives when things are going well.	DO crank up the positive recognition when good behavior is occurring. If you use positive recognition only to suppress bad behavior, your children will pick up on this, and you'll get more bad behavior. Kids know where the juice is!
DON'T turn away and ignore a broken rule. A foot on the line is a foot on the line. Even a tiny bit of a threat or aggression or arguing is still a broken rule.	DO maintain a high standard for desired behavior. Never waver when it's enforcement time.

DON'T remind children of the rules: "Remember, no feet on the furniture. Hey, didn't I just say *no feet on the furniture?*"	DO give time-outs consistently and with no reminders or warnings. If you find yourself repeating a rule, it's time to start enforcing it. If you find yourself thinking, "My children have forgotten the rules," your enforcement needs to be stricter – and you need to make a point of celebrating when that rule is *not being broken.* Keep commending your children for even the smallest degrees of appropriate effort, attitude and action.

The two main reasons that conventional consequences fail: First, they are given "uncleanly," muddied with parents' emotional attachment to the rules being followed by way of the gift of relationship at he wrong time; and second, because the time-in – the "in-the-game" feeling of success – is not strong enough. Unclean, emotionally loaded consequences are confusing to children. And if the game isn't exciting, if that isn't really where all the great action is, children can feel like they're missing out on something, and they may turn to rule-breaking.

Time-out is not a punishment. Time-out is a kind and unceremonious result of a rule being broken. It's a message to the child that says, "Here's a chance to check yourself…to control your impulses and get back in the game, where all the juice is." This consequence has the "kiss of forgiveness" built right in; by design, it moves the child right back into success.

I contend that lack of forgiveness is holding onto the past in thoughts, energies or actions. True forgiveness is demonstrated by "energetically" moving on cleanly to the next NOW.

If another rule is broken, administer another time-out/reset to give the child a chance to get himself back under control. Do it as many times as you need to. Make no reference to whether the child has already gotten a time-out. *Stay in the moment.*

Redirection: More Energy for Poor Choices

Positive discipline for preschoolers almost always involves the tool of *redirection*: the child is directed away from an activity where rules are being broken (or are about to be) and into a more suitable activity. Two- to five-year-olds are generally considered to be too young to be disciplined in any other way. But from the Nurtured Heart "energy" standpoint, using this tactic is tantamount to starting these preschoolers on the $100-for-poor-choices gravy train.

Let's say your preschooler is playing with his friend while you're engaged in some paperwork at your desk in the next room. Your son decides to see what happens if he smacks his buddy. The friend's screeching draws you to the scene. You find out what happened and take your child aside, speaking to him gently about how he mustn't hit and how it's wrong and not nice to the friend. Or perhaps you offer a few stern, highly energized words about how he must not hit. Then you take him to a cool new activity and stay until he's engaged in it. Your child plays peacefully for a bit but then starts to get bored. He is now once again craving that attention and energy from his "favorite toy." He gets it by...smacking his buddy again.

Preschoolers are just as good at seeing the relationship between rule-breaking and adult relationship as older children are. Children under five need *lots* of adult attention and have less internal self-control. From the perspective this approach, redirection is yet another wheelbarrow full of relationship at the wrong moment in time: when a rule has been broken.

The good news: Young children respond beautifully as soon as energy is directed at them in response to rules *not* being broken and other messages of positivity.

With preschoolers, a 10- to 15-second time-out, followed immediately by a rich time-in, works much better than redirection for encouraging good choices. Young children respond especially well to "reset" as a substitute for time-out. Another option is to use the terms "red light" and "green light" or "pause" and "play" for time-out and time-in. These are different names for the same concept and the same intervention.

Tucson Head Start and the Nurtured Heart Approach: An Amazing Success Story

Several years ago, I gave a presentation on my approach to a group of parents and teachers in Tucson, Arizona. Afterward, several attendees approached and told me they worked for the Head Start program.

Head Start is a preschool program for underprivileged, at-risk families whose children are more likely to face behavioral issues, psychiatric diagnoses and medication. In Tucson at that time, Head Start had an entire mental health department just for all the behavioral health issues (such as attention deficit-hyperactivity disorder) so common in those classrooms. Many additional referrals were being made by Head Start to outside mental health providers for evaluation, diagnosis and treatment.

Head Start staff's interest in the Nurtured Heart Approach rested primarily on its potential to help their most difficult students. I was willing to try to help, but only if they were willing to use the approach with all students, not just the most intense students. They agreed.

In preparation for my observing and working in the classrooms, Head Start teachers gave me packets full of research materials used as foundations for their current disciplinary approaches. Reading through those materials, I was hardly surprised that they were dealing with out-of-control classrooms. Redirection was their main disciplinary technique. They had tried the "minute per year" approach to time-out, and it hadn't worked. Combined with other discouraging experiences with traditional approaches, they had dismissed the time-out as ineffective.

I began by doing a whole-class intervention using the Nurtured Heart Approach while Head Start staff watched and studied what I was doing. They read my book *Transforming the Difficult Child* to learn more about the approach. Within a week, in each of 10 problematic classrooms, things had turned around. Often, staff found that the children with the worst behavior had turned around the most and were displaying the *best* behavior – a change I could have predicted, knowing what those worst-behaved kids were looking for and knowing that intensity can be the driving force of greatness as easily as it can manifest in difficulty. Many observers watched this whole process, and there was agreement that the "non-challenging" children were flourishing, too.

The benefits were so clear that Tucson Head Start arranged a one-day session in which I trained teachers from 80 classrooms. Supervisors of Tucson Head Start became experts in the approach and helped implement it throughout all the centers.

In the first year the Nurtured Heart Approach was applied at Tucson Head Start, there was not a single ADHD-related diagnosis. In the seven years that followed, the success record held: not a single child had been placed on medications for behavioral problems. Huge amounts of money were saved on mental health services, and with that extra money, the system was able to increase enrollment from about 2,000 to 3,000 children.

I attribute this great story to Head Start's willingness to revamp their practices. They not only changed the trajectory of the messages of success they were sending the children, but they made a commitment to not energizing negativity and to having a new and simpler form of reset that served them and ultimately the children more perfectly.

The New Time-Out and the Intention of Clarity

I used to believe that it was crucial for a child to actually move to a time-out location, such as a chair. I used to recommend an elaborate plan in case the child refused to go to time-out when told. I honestly no longer feel that is crucial in the home setting. What follows is an explanation that will help you see what it took me some time to recognize.

Think about the video game example that I described earlier. In those games, a child is sitting at a console or monitor, focused on the primary goal of getting higher and higher scores and levels of attainment. Occasionally the child breaks a rule of the game, and when he does, the game unfailingly delivers a consequence. I want to point out a few interesting things about this process.

Adults look at those consequences and think, "Oh my gosh, how drastic and disgusting – blood spurting, heads rolling!" But ask any child: he'll tell you that the consequence is really nothing. He's back in the game in a matter of seconds. Even if the last penalty ended the game, he just starts up a new round.

So, first and foremost, the consequence is really a matter of the child's perception of having had a reset. Ask anyone who plays these games – they want only to be back in the game. They really feel the brief consequence as meaningful – but not scary or punitive.

And somehow, because the game so highly energizes successes and has such clear limits and consequences, all the child can think about is trying to be the world's best player. HE GETS GREAT AT NOT BREAKING THE RULES. It becomes a skill in and of itself and he chooses to not break rules, *of his own volition*. No one is forcing him or standing over him. No one is telling him he has to be good at this. He has the illusion of having accepted and completed the consequence because the game allows him right back in. And – here's the kicker – *he doesn't ever have to leave his seat to have this perception and for it to be superbly effective at inspiring success.*

The time-out recommended in these pages is the simplest road I could find to creating a parallel process in which the child is led to believe the consequence is successfully over and that he is back in the game.

If the child "appears" to have refused the consequence, simply turn away for a bit. When the moment feels right, turn back and announce that the consequence is over; then, stay vigilant for the next opportunity to praise good choices. The very best way to declare that the child is back in the game is to show your energy for his success as soon as possible in relation to not breaking the very rule that had earned the time-out and for good choices in general.

In the early days of developing this approach, I also felt that bigger infractions deserved a time-out plus some level of community service when the initial reset was over. I no longer feel that this is crucial because, as in the video game analogy, the goal is not to measure off the perfect punishment that will awaken the child to not wanting to break rules ever again. What really wins the day is to move the child into a whole new way of living. My experience is that this is best accomplished by relentlessly moving the child into deeper versions of success. The child who transforms is really awakening to her greatness; she then wants to manifest that in every way possible. That's the sweet outcome I have seen over and over again.

I daresay, based on my own parenting experience and my work with thousands of other parents, what parents really want is a child who *wants* to be the best in the world because it feels good to him to exercise his greatness...a child who, of his own volition, wants to NOT break the rules.

I don't think we want future generations of fear-based children who are forever terrified of mistakes and transgressions. The latter can only live a shadow of a fulfilled life, always walking on eggshells and unable to fully experience the joy of living.

Sibling Rivalry and the CSI

Any parent with more than one child knows that sibling rivalry can be a major source of grief in the family. Traditional methods are a set-up when it comes to sibling rivalry. When our beloved children are at each other's throats, our desire to referee and mediate and accidentally give the problem lots of juice is hard to resist. The Nurtured Heart Approach can help you deal with this problem more constructively.

Let's say sisters Annie and Josie start out fighting over a favorite game and soon escalate into hitting each other. The temptation of the parent might be to do a little crime scene investigation (CSI) to see who started it, who should get the game, and who deserves a steeper consequence.

Here's how to handle it with this approach: Since both are fighting, both get a time-out for breaking a rule. Then, praise them both for sitting through their brief reset and stay nearby as they begin to interact again.

Let's say Annie remarks, with an angry flourish, "Here, Josie, *you can have* the stupid game." That's your signal to jump in and acknowledge her action: "Annie, I see that even though you really wanted to play with that game, you let your little sister use it first. That's so considerate of you. I appreciate your maturity!"

This example demonstrates the "win-win" nature of the Nurtured Heart Approach. The parent gets to move steadfastly into the next moment of success, setting the stage for that moment with the time-out/reset; she is able to deliver her heart's message in a digestible, positive manner. The children get fast closure for problems and a seamless transition to positivity.

Here's one more example: James and Chris both want to choose the movie for family video night. In a flash, they are at one another, making threats and calling each other names. In the past, their parents would have escalated along with them, yelling that it's not okay to argue and use bad words. They would have mounted an intensive CSI to "get to the bottom of the issue" – to find out *why* the boys were making these poor choices.

After taking a class in the Nurtured Heart Approach, these parents have a whole new way of coping with sibling rivalry. One parent simply says, "That's a consequence," and both turn away for less than a minute (not requiring the children to go to any special chairs). They then turn back and create closure, with one parent saying, "Great job, boys, getting that consequence done so well. I really appreciate that you have stopped arguing. Thanks for following that rule. Now I need you both to quickly collaborate and make a decision. Whoever doesn't get their preference this time will get to choose next time." Within a minute the boys reach a decision, allowing both parents to further commend their sons for great collaboration and choosing to work things out. A win-win for all, with no need for the CSI and no incidence of accidental reward.

Consequences: Building Greatness

One can have a good life without purpose, but without purpose one will never experience the beauty of a great life. Conversely, with a life of great purpose, you can have a less than perfect existence but still feel tremendous fulfillment. Through living a life of purpose, you help so many others manifest greatness: by being your own greatness, you draw others into your inspired energy field.

Consequences are an extremely important window of opportunity to support children in finding and fulfilling their purpose. A child exposed to clear limits and clear results will eventually internalize great clarity and a great sense of order; these are of vital importance in identifying and fulfilling one's purpose in life.

Children no longer fight rules and consequences once they learn that the rule boundaries are solid and that the consequences for breaking rules are nothing to fear – but that they also hold no attraction. They not only live with them: they *collaborate* with them. They fully accept the way the environment is organized and use the rules to focus their efforts toward mastery and achievement.

Focused effort is a trait of greatness, and once the issue of rules is no longer an obstacle, the child can apply this trait to catapult from level to level and experience the fun of attainment.

Confusing limits and punitive, escalating consequences draw children toward the energetic $100 bills that flow when rules are broken. That will never lead to order, organization and clarity. It will lead to sadness and confusion – not qualities of greatness but obstacles to greatness.

Clear, clean limits and consequences are a gift that brings simplicity to a child. Simplicity is yet one more gift of greatness, as is the greatness of closure: that there is always a result of a violation or a mistake, but it has an end...and on the other side is yet more success – often, greater levels of success than ever before.

The "kiss" of forgiveness that is inherent in being welcomed back into the game by way of these further successes is perhaps the greatest gift of all. This kind of forgiveness lends sweetness to the heart, opening it to new beginnings.

Time-Out, Warnings and Leaking Negativity

Leaks of negativity tend to spring forth quite readily when it's consequence time, or when parents see that rule breaking is about to transpire. Let's look at how this can happen and how you can maintain Stand III when giving a time-out or during the time when a child is approaching the line between rules not broken and rules broken.

Remember: everyone gives energy to negativity from time to time. You will find yourself doing so more often when you first begin the approach. Then, as you refine your unique version, you'll see more and more clearly where you're leaking. In many cases, your children's response to you will illuminate those leaks and help you figure out how to give your energy to positivity instead.

Here are a few of the most common negativity leaks. When you catch yourself in any of these, stop, take a breath, and get your three-legged table (each leg = one of the three Stands) strong again. This means returning to reflections of the positive, withdrawing energy from negative choices, and strictly enforcing the rules.

When you catch yourself leaking negativity, don't try to fix what's already been said – just move into the next moment with your Stands intact.

Stern looks of warning.

What parent hasn't done this? It's probably the most common leak of all. Your child is about to break a rule or is in the process of breaking a rule; you catch her eyes with yours and give her 'The Look.'

It's intended to say, "You'd better not do what I think you're about to do," or "You'd better knock that off *right now!*"

You may as well hand the child a gilded invitation that reads, "I non-verbally invite you to press the button that makes the fireworks go off." By throwing 'The Look,' *you are also advertising your personal, emotional investment in the rules being followed.* This is a major source of negativity.

In trying to prevent the child from breaking a rule – in giving a warning – you are working against the truth of the matter, which is that you cannot prevent a child from breaking a rule.

Warnings of any kind are commensurate with inadvertently energizing negativity. You are giving some degree of energy and relationship in the context of the child's poor choice.

Instead of a warning, give an unceremonious reset, and have that be a bridge to the next NOW of positive choice – a means of alerting the child to his greatness.

"You're doing great, but I need you to .... (i.e., do even better than you're currently doing)."

See the leak? Your message might seem positive, but you're pointing out the lack; in doing so, you're taking the wind out of the positive reflection's sails.

Would you give your child a beautifully wrapped box containing something he doesn't want? Would you give him some unpleasant-tasting but nice-looking cake and tell him, "Here's some cake, but it tastes pretty bad"? Would you say, "I love you, but if you start making your bed in the mornings, I'll love you even more"? Of course not. A positive reflection should never have a "but..." attached to it.

Any kind of energy and relationship in the context of negativity, no matter how well it's gift-wrapped, is still going to undermine your overarching intention of bringing your child to a new sense of inner wealth and greatness.

Comparing siblings to one another in a way that is denigrating to one sibling.

For example, you say "Your brother has HIS homework done" to his sister, who's not staying as focused and so is taking longer to finish.

164

This might seem like a positive reflection of the brother, but you're being strongly negative toward his sister in the process.

Reinforce the brother: "I see you've finished your homework already. You stayed really focused and got it done – that's showing great perseverance. Awesome work." The sister will hear what you're saying, believe me. And when she finally finishes, reflect her achievement, too: "I could see that it was hard for you to stay focused, but you hung in there. Now you're all done, and you've fulfilled your responsibility. That's real dedication. Great job."

Giving a time-out in a stern, accusatory or angry tone.

Remember, you are de-energizing negativity. You have no emotional stake in the rules being followed. Snapping "Okay – *that's* a time-out!!" at a child who has broken the rule means you're giving him those $100 bills. You're letting him push your buttons. For time-outs to truly work, your child has to see irrefutably that there's no longer any gain for negativity.

"Wow – even Tommy *is helping with the chores today!"*

Subtext: Tommy never helps with the chores. He gives everyone a hard time when he's asked to help with the chores. Actually, he enjoys starting messy projects while everyone else is trying to clean up. And look, today he's helping! Am I dreaming?

This is not positive reflection, nor is it staying in the moment. Even if you think you are witnessing a miracle akin to the parting of the Red Sea, *don't respond like this to your child.* He'll feel shamed, as though he can't escape the pattern of negative behavior. The above remark reflects being at least partially in the past, not truly in the moment. Stay in the present and celebrate the choice he is making in this very moment.

"Wowyrgreat" (positive words tossed out at lightning speed)

A genuine positive reflection can't be hurried. This doesn't mean it has to take a long time; you'll get to the point where these reflections flow easily and where they are virtually always clear, energized and specific. Until then, take the few extra seconds to put it all together in your mind and give your reflections in a measured, focused, clear way so that the child doesn't end up feeling like you're just try-ing to control his behavior with disingenuous remarks.

"Come on, kids, we're almost done!" (Or: "We're almost there," or some other statement that comes across like a pep talk instead of a positive recognition)

Let's say you're trying to get the table cleared and the dishes done with your children's help. They've been doing well so far, and you're feeling like you can let up on the positives. Then you notice a few clues that the wheels are about to fall off: Betsy starts drifting off to-ward the TV, hoping you won't notice; Cameron starts using the wooden spoons to drum on the trash can rather than putting them away. You exhort them with words designed to get them back on track – and they quickly leap into rule breaking. What happened?

First, make sure that no rule is being broken. If no one has crossed the line and no time-outs are required, swallow the warning you might feel tempted to spout, and remember: Until inner wealth is solid and has a life of its own, it's too soon for you to let up on the positives.

Your children needed the recognitions to keep flowing in order to stay focused on how successful they were being in helping you out. The next thing that happened was a leak of negativity in the form of the mini-pep talk, where you essentially voiced your concern that they might not stick with it. Exasperation is a negativity leak. Don't go there. Instead, get the positives flowing again. Now would be a good time for what Nurtured Heart trainer Tom Grove calls "no-fail directives": give each child a task at which he or she is highly unlikely to fail.

For example, you could say to Betsy, "I think I hear the TV. I need you to go and make sure it's turned off and then come back and help me dry these pots." Tell Cameron, "That's great musical accompani-ment! I want you to play for me until I finish drying this platter, then go and put those spoons in the drawer." When they do as they're told, pour on the positives again. It's time-in!

Telling the child you're sorry that you have to give a time-out or other consequence; or patting the child or otherwise trying to comfort the child when a consequence is delivered.

If you recall your parents telling you, "This hurts me as much as it hurts you" when they punished you, you know how hollow *that* statement can be!

You do not have to commiserate with a child who has broken a rule. Doing so will give the child the impression that you have an emotional attachment to the rules being followed. Let the time-out be neutral and un-emotional. Don't apologize to the child for enforcing the rules. Let the reset/time-out happen and jump back into time-in.

Remember: time-out is an illusion. It's a reset, not a punishment, and there's nothing to fear in it, for you or the child.

Threatening the child with a time-out.

"If you do that again, you'll get a time-out!" This warning breaks off all three legs of the three-legged table. It gives relationship to negativity, it avoids strictness, and it doesn't energize positive choices. It also displays your emotional attachment to the rules being followed. Either a rule is broken or it isn't. If it is, give the time-out and get ready to propel the next time-in.

If a rule hasn't been broken, the child is still in the game of success, thus far having chosen not to break the rule. You can commend that choice, because we all know the line could be crossed at any moment. The child skimming away from rule breaking is like the player with the ball who manages to avoid going out of bounds. Sometimes those plays get the loudest applause.

Having lower standards for one sibling who has "special needs."

It's true that difficult or intense children need a more intense application of this approach – but equally strict enforcement of rules is imperative for every child in your household.

The intense, difficult or disabled (learning disabled, mentally ill or physically disabled) child needs stronger and more frequent positives, but he does not need different rules, special exceptions or warnings. The rules are the rules for everyone, and you can have very high standards in the rules you set as long as you *never waver when it's time to enforce.*

Children have an amazing way of complying with your expectations. If you reveal that you expect a child to screw up – for example, by giving him a warning, a "look" or some even subtler message about that expectation – the child is likely to do what you expect him to do. If you shine out that you know that every one of your children is great and equally capable of following the rules, they tend to comply with *that* expectation. Our society so often dilutes expectations for children with disabilities; as soon as the limits become fuzzy, the child quickly comes to see that dancing around and across the line leads to connection and relationship. Big leaks ensue.

It may take some time and effort on your part to stop revealing, through emotions or body language, that you expect less from one of your children than from the others, but until you do so, you'll be giving energy to negativity.

Once you get in the habit of giving consequences cleanly, and for even the most miniscule bit of rule breaking, you will find that leaks happen much less often.

Strictness and High Expectations

Strictness is not about being punitive or frightening to your children. It's about keeping the standard for desired behavior very high. It's about never wavering when it comes time to enforce a rule. Hold every child to the same standards, regardless of what has happened in the past.

Make your children as responsible as you can for their own actions. Make them think as much as possible. In my opinion, this is best achieved not by discussing and mediating problems as they occur, but by observing carefully and pointing out positive thinking and actions. When you see them choosing to avoid problems, clearly "accuse" them of doing so, and be crystal clear about how you've seen them making positive choices.

This creates a kind of accountability that lets your child know you believe in her. It lets her know that you count on her to address and solve her own problems and that you will make sure she experiences success when she does. Shine forth your faith in their competency in navigating their own lives. Be respectful, and make clear that their behavior is their decision. This can all be better accomplished by pointing out when competency is occurring and by avoiding the pitfalls of trying to teach competency when it isn't happening.

As you try to work with this approach, keep in mind the image of the three-legged table. If you lose a leg temporarily, work like crazy to keep the other two standing. Don't be in a hurry to solve the problem or straighten everybody out; your rush gives power to problems. If you keep that positivity leg standing, the answers will emerge.

CHAPTER SEVEN

Problems and Solutions

Amanda was a mother who had read my books and was considering implementing the Nurtured Heart Approach with her children but was on the fence about it. Her children weren't particularly difficult; they certainly weren't candidates for a behavioral diagnosis. Traditional disciplinary methods had worked decently, but Amanda wanted to go to that next level of consciously cultivating the greatness she could see blossoming in her children.

She was tired of threatening, bargaining and lecturing; she felt overwrought and wanted a happier, more positive environment at home. But she was still stuck in her old programming and unable to release it enough to plunge fully into the new approach.

We communicated, and she told me a story that I've heard, in various permutations, dozens of times over the years. "My son goes to preschool," she told me, "and he had been having trouble in a few areas – specifically, not sitting still during group time, refusing to do lessons with the teacher, and pouring his juice out on the ground outside instead of drinking it. So the teacher recommended that I start what she called a 'star system' – a credit system to help motivate him to do better.

"I did implement a basic system: I told him he had to sit still and be quiet during circle time; he had to do a lesson with the teacher; and he could not dump his juice or yogurt on the ground. If he didn't follow those rules, he would not get a sticker on the calendar that day. I tried to make the rules negative, and didn't succeed too well in that at first. I tried to give him not only stickers (which he could accrue to earn a trip to the toy store for an inexpensive toy) but also lots of positive reinforcement for all he was doing right.

"It was working well. He got stickers for a couple of days, and then didn't get one, and so he got to have that experience too – and it motivated him to reach those goals the next day. Then, a few days after

I'd started the sticker program, his teacher approached me at the end of the school day. She was waffling about whether it was a 'star day' – he had followed the rules we had already set up, albeit with some boundary pushing, but had not broken any of the rules. That was a real eye opener to me," Amanda noted, "that *she didn't know* whether it was a star day or not. Clearly, the line between rules broken and rules followed was unclear in *her* mind.

"I told her we'd start adding rules and if he didn't break them he'd get his sticker. I told her I would be adding 'no pushing' to the list. She said, 'Oh, no, no, no! That's so *negative*. Try something positive, like 'when you feel like pushing, use your words instead,' but her version was about twice that long.

"That's when it really hit me," Amanda told me, "the incredible vagueness and verboseness of so-called 'positive discipline.' What does a child make of rules like 'use your words?' I totally got why it doesn't work. A child faced with a rule like that really doesn't know where the line is, and he can see that the teacher doesn't know, either!

"I hate to admit it, but I got a little snappish with this teacher. She just seemed so *sure* of her approach. And I had seen what went on in that school – by and large those kids were *not* being disciplined very effectively.

"I answered, 'First of all, that seems like too many words. Why not keep it simple and straightforward? No pushing. Ever. It's never okay to push. What's wrong with making a negative rule for a negative behavior?'

"She continued to argue for a 'positive' rule, but I couldn't be swayed. I had this vivid mental picture of my son literally standing near a big, fuzzy line drawn on the ground, inching ever closer, looking around…and of this teacher hovering nearby, exhorting him not to get too close. How close is too close? What a confusing mess!

"Finally, she told me that I knew my son best and should do what I felt was best for him. And when I walked away from that conversation, I finally understood in my bones why the Nurtured Heart Approach is best for him and for my daughter as well."

So-called positive discipline and the Nurtured Heart Approach are both effective, in the way that both fast-food burgers and a healthful salad are both food. They may both be enough to sustain us. They can both taste good. But the nutrition they provide is hardly comparable. And over the course of a lifetime, which do you think is going to enable one to thrive instead of just survive?

In this chapter, we'll look at a few of the most common issues parents encounter when first attempting to put the Nurtured Heart Approach in motion. Dealing with teachers and even with co-parents who either don't "get" the Nurtured Heart mindset or who don't have any desire to change their ways is one very common issue. Let's start there.

Q: If I implement the Nurtured Heart Approach and my child's teachers or my spouse won't, how do I handle it?

A: A child who is nurtured with this approach at home – particularly a child who is not having significant disciplinary problems in school – will probably do fine in a traditional school setting. Still, my goal is to paint a network of positivity and appreciation of greatness that's big enough to include every child, and you can help by letting your child's teacher(s) know what you're up to at home.

My approach is being implemented by teachers, administrators, whole schools and even whole school *systems*; it might be worth your while to let your child's teachers (or even the principal of the school) know that this approach is available to them.

The book I wrote with Tom Grove, *The Inner Wealth Initiative: The Nurtured Heart Approach for Educators*, is a good start, and they can visit difficultchild.com for more support and information about workshops and trainings.

If your spouse or co-parent is resistant to using the approach, your own efforts can end up being undermined. Here are a few tips to help you succeed anyhow – and, perhaps, to win your partner over to your way of thinking:

- Plow ahead with the approach. Throw your heart and soul into it. Keep your positivity shining; don't give in to negative energy; and be unflinchingly strict. Don't give your partner the opportunity to enter into negative relationship with the kids. The power of the approach might be enough to convince your partner to slide right in beside you on the greatness train.

(Resist any impulse to say "I told you so!" That's some serious negativity!) But if that doesn't happen, forge ahead yourself. One parent using the approach is much better than none.

- Shine the approach on your partner, even as you do so with your children. Build his or her inner wealth.
- Bribe, cajole or persuade your partner, by any means necessary, to simply give the approach a try for two or three weeks just to see what the effects are. If he or she rejects reading the book, offer to coach him or her on the basics and to help all along the way; or order a DVD or CD from difficultchild.com.
- As you begin seeing your positive influence unfold, your voice will get stronger and your ability to tell your truth and ask for what you want will grow. If need be, ask your partner to let you be the primary parent for now and to stand back for a time. I've seen parents who enact this approach get so strong in their conviction that this is benefiting their child that they wind up getting what they want from their spouse – even though this initially seemed unimaginable.

The next book I'm planning to write is about the application and impact of this approach on adults: specifically, how adults can use it *on themselves* to become their *greatest selves*. My hope is to get that book into the hands of adults who have never experienced an environment where their inner wealth was actively cultivated. For so many parents, their childhood memories and default mode of parenting involve shaming, arguing, threatening and criticism. These elements can be flushed away by the power of the greatness already residing within them. This book will, I hope, be a valuable tool for parents (and teachers) who need an extra boost in their own inner wealth as they shine that light of positivity on their children.

Q: My children are doing OK with "normal" approaches, but the Nurtured Heart Approach really attracts me. How can I make the leap?

A: Getting and staying motivated to use this approach is usually easy for parents of difficult children. They're at the end of their rope and are looking for a solution that works; their sanity often feels dependent on it. On the other hand, parents whose children are generally well-behaved – "normal" – may have a harder time pushing through their own resistance (and that of their children) to reinvent their parenting approach, and may give up before digging in far enough to see the benefits.

The best reason for all parents to use this approach can be summed up with a single (and, to many parents, terrifying) word: *adolescence*.

Even so-called "perfect" children can have a rough time when those early teen years come around. Middle-school-aged children can experience a thrashing of their self-esteem and confidence, and we take it for granted that the trials and tribulations of children in this age group are par for the course.

In her hilarious memoir of parenting, *Operating Instructions: A Journal of My Son's First Year*, Anne Lamott describes the difficult years of her own early adolescence, years when she recalls her and her peers being "emotionally broken by unrequited love and at the same time amped out of our minds on hormones and shame":

> One descended from the relative safety and wildness and bigness one felt in sixth grade, eleven years old. Then the worm turned, and it was all over for any small feeling that one was essentially all right. One wasn't...Seventh and eighth grades...were about violence, meanness, chaos... they were about feeling completely other. But more than anything else, they were about hurt and aloneness. (p.10-11)

Teens are growing up in a world where knowing one's purpose and value is increasingly difficult. A child who has been "hijacked" into his own greatness from an early age is far more likely to negotiate the standard "'tween" and teen obstacles with grace and poise. That child is more likely to avoid the pitfalls of drugs, teen pregnancy and peer pressures to do things he knows are wrong. A child who grows up in the light of greatness will want to stay focused on what's important while still having balance and fun. He will possess the inherent ability to choose friends and situations that dovetail with that spirit of greatness.

What will seventh and eighth grades be like without all that shame, violence and chaos? (Not much can be done about the hormones, of course, but the effects of surging hormones in an environment of inner wealth will not elicit cruelty to others, but understanding and empathy toward one's self and others who are on the same rollercoaster.) What will a world made by children who are rich with inner wealth look and feel like? I hope to see it in my lifetime – because I know it will be absolutely amazing.

Q: I feel like I'm doing everything right, but it's not working: my children aren't responding to the approach. How might I be going wrong?

A: Some of the most common reasons for this are:

- your rates of recognition are too low;
- your recognitions are not powerful (detailed and specific) enough;
- you aren't delivering them with enough energy;
- you are enforcing rules vaguely;
- you are accidentally energizing negativity – "leaking" negativity.

In many instances, parents who come to me with this issue have the basic strategies in place; but I can see that they will have to "crank it up" to fit the life force of their child. Many children simply need a stronger version. Once the parents amp up their application of the approach, the results are usually remarkable. It's not unusual for me to advise a parent to apply the approach "like your life depended upon it." In a way, at least qualitatively, it does.

The other common reason that things fail to fall into place is this: *trying to integrate this approach into the myriad other approaches that you have studied or learned to use over the years.*

Concerned parents who want to "do parenting right" often are on the lookout for advice and techniques wherever they can find them. Bits of advice culled from a few pages of a book, from an e-mail from another parent, from teachers or from magazines can be influential for parents who are seeking answers. Loyalties are formed to "pieces of approaches" – and those allegiances often are hard to step away from when a new, more comprehensive approach enters the picture. Unfortunately, most of those pieces run counter to this approach and undermine its effect. I am astounded at how often this is the case.

My recommendation – and one that has worked like a charm – is to *temporarily put all other methods aside, no matter how meaningful they have been to you.* Once you can do this, you will start to get a true picture of how the Nurtured Heart Approach hangs together on its own, and you'll glimpse the beginnings of an inner realization of why it works and what is at stake. Having made that leap, you will then have a great perspective of what parts of other approaches can fit with and support what you are accomplishing – and which parts are better abandoned.

Q: Does it matter when I start using this approach?

A: You can start when children are infants, as I did with my daughter; this is the best option if it's available to you. An infant or very young child will have no resistance at all to your positive reflections.

This being said, know that you can start at any point in the child's life – even grown children can benefit. The older the child is when you begin, the more ingrained will be their attachment to the way things have always been. The older or adult child may be more resistant to your positive reflections and your cultivation of their greatness than would be the case for a younger child. Bear in mind, however, that once the child comes to trust the new you who reflects positivity and cherishes greatness, the resistance stops.

If your child is past elementary-school age when you begin, be prepared for bigger and deeper efforts in applying the approach. Refer back to the three Stands. The older the child, the more likely it is he will initially test or resist you as you implement the approach. Take this as a sign that it's working and that he feels the difference but just doesn't quite yet trust that he can keep you connected without reverting to negativity. Use that as evidence of a need to apply the approach with a stronger trajectory.

Q: My 11-year-old is really resisting the positives I'm trying to pour over him. He's even trying to get me to go back to the negative

ways by insulting me in very hurtful, personal ways. How do I cope and move through this?

A: Your child knows you better than almost anyone. It follows that he knows your weaknesses – the tender spots where you can be wounded and thus pushed into giving him that fireworks show he craves and finds so comforting.

Have a rule such as "No insulting others." (And don't get into a battle with the child over what is and isn't an insult. You both know.) When your child insults you, simply give him a reset; or at the most, "Wow, you have incredible perception into people. Reset." Although you may feel hurt by the child's jab, don't show it; simply issue an un-energized time-out. Show the child that you can manage strong feelings and maintain your positive focus.

The real key is in staying true to this moment and the next moments to follow. The real transformation rests on how you respond after the reset by then applauding the new, great decision not to insult. That's when you can fold the very same "lecture" energy into a beneficial rant: "How great it is that you are now handling your feelings well by not insulting and by not being disrespectful!" Then, amp it up by saying any number of related things that honor the truth of the new NOW. For example: "Louisa, I really appreciate the greatness you are showing in being considerate right now." Or "Matti, the good judgment you are using right now to be nice is a quality of greatness that I really appreciate in you."

Q: We have big battles over bedtime at our house. When they're doing well, I say something like, "Now THIS is what you should do when I say it's time for bed. This is great!" Then, everything falls apart. What did I do wrong?

A: Your children are finally moving through the bed-time routine more or less without fuss and independently; they aren't fighting or moaning that they don't want to brush their teeth; they're doing everything in the right order. You shout the above statement out in your effort to reinforce them, and the order quickly turns to mayhem. What went wrong?

You're shaming them by comparing their behavior in this moment to their behavior in the past. You're using the "should" term instead of reflecting, in vivid detail, what is happening in the moment. By leaving out the details (how Jenna is brushing her teeth so thoroughly, demonstrating respect for her own body and her health; how James is neatly putting his dirty clothes in the hamper, being helpful and considerate by taking initiative to keep the home neat and tidy), you imply that all you really want is to keep everyone in line. Be specific and personal holding the bigger purpose – to build your children's greatness. I'm really saying let your child see how open your heart is to enjoying her greatness by giving your appreciation a voice.

Q: I try to keep the positives coming, but sometimes my anger takes over and I lose it and start yelling. I hit the boiling point and then I feel like a failure.

A: Empathize with yourself before you respond to something that angers you. Take a few breaths – tell the child to wait if you have to – and tell yourself (silently) about your own feelings. "I am so angry right now!" Then, step out of your immediate emotional response. Say to yourself: "When he used to do this, I would fall into the trap and go right into the drama. He needs to experience that this will not happen, despite my feeling angry."

Remember: the child is trying to drive you to your boiling point because he has always been energetically fed by that escalation and explosion with relationship, connection and response. Also keep in mind that rule breaking on the part of the child is not a personal affront to you. He's after your energy and presence, that's all. Show him that rule breaking isn't the way to get it. It leads only to a consequence, not to $100 bills.

Then, to arrive at the transformation you really want in the future, work even more vehemently to show him that relationship is there, but only in connection to all the great things he is doing. *However, do not dangle that carrot and say that will happen IF or WHEN he is great.* You must irrefutably show him that he is being great *in this moment,* and he will feel the relationship, love and intimacy inherent in that exchange.

Nowhere in this approach is there any denial of emotion or any Polyanna pretense that all is happy no matter what. Acknowledge to yourself, "Yes, I feel livid, but I'm not going to send this message to my child." Your anger is not you, and you don't have to act on it. Translate your anger and fear into a fierce resolve to overwhelm your child with evidence of his greatness.

If you find yourself losing your temper, give *yourself* a reset! Let your child know that you're doing this. He's likely to be impressed.

Q: What if I give a reset and my child won't do it?

A: Don't get into any discussion about it. That would be giving energy to negativity.

Instead, relay to your child the "illusion" that she has indeed completed the consequence – even though she doesn't think she has. You could walk away for a minute and come back, having avoided falling into the trap of responding to the refusal...and more often than not, you can declare that the child has, in fact, completed the time-out. Say, "Nicole, thanks for getting your consequence done. It's over and now you aren't arguing. I appreciate the good choice you are making."

Don't warn her, and ignore her complaints and arguments that she did it or was about to do it. The stricter you are in a clean way, the sooner she'll learn to just get the reset out of the way. Think video game therapy.

If you do feel that you need to use a back-up consequence, removing a privilege often works well (no TV or computer time for a certain period, for example); in schools, the consequence for refusing a reset is usually a detention.

Q: My daughter is often sarcastic and complains a lot. Should I consequence her for her attitude?

A: Attitude is a slippery slope. Sarcasm, "annoying" behaviors, fussiness, complaining and smart aleck remarks are best ignored, unless a rule has clearly been broken.

The reason is that defining these behaviors and remarks clearly is difficult. If you are being disrespected and you have a rule against that, administer a consequence, as you would do for any rule broken; but be clear, within yourself, what exactly that rule means or encompasses. If the child is exhibiting just a show of attitude or sarcasm, let it go and look for the positive. Let the child see that you can't be moved from your focus on the good stuff and can't be pulled into responding to negativity.

It can hurt when your child hollers out something like, "I hate you!" or "Don't touch me!" Try to use Experiential Recognition: "Wow, I can see that you are having some strong feelings right now, and you're doing your best to express that. Great honesty." If attitude is really bothering you, or you want the child to further express what's going on, you can say to the child, "You need to rephrase that" or "I need you to find another way to say what you're feeling." If your child calls you a name or curses at you, however, the line has been crossed, and a reset is in order.

The important thing here is that you distinguish for yourself where the line is. Be true to when the line is touched or crossed and administer a reset. When the child is upset but has avoided touching or crossing the line, the truth may be that he is restraining himself from violating a rule that he could be breaking. There's your window to appreciation!

I know I am grateful when my child is angry yet not breaking rules. Anger is human and is not the enemy. *Acting out* anger is where I draw the line. The truth is that handling anger well can be a trait of greatness and can propel a person to great creativity and great achievements.

Q: Should I post the house rules?

A: Are the rules posted at the sidelines of the basketball court? Do tennis players refer to their crib notes in the middle of a match to make sure they know them all? How about those big fellows on the football field: Do you see them referring to notes just in case they forget the rules? Of course not! They know them cold, and when they forget or ignore one, they're reminded with a brief reset. The same goes for video games: No kid reads the rules through and refers back to them as they play – they just dive in and learn as they go. Similarly, this is the way you can apply your house rules in the context of this approach.

I've always maintained that it isn't necessary to set rules in any official way. You don't have to wait for a rule to be officially set, re-layed to each child and written on the list before you can enforce it.

You can let the experience of following the rules – and your reflection of this back to the child – be the teacher of the rules. Posting them is optional.

A need for a new rule might emerge on the fly. If you sense that a new one has been broken, give a reset – even if the rule in question has never previously been stated to the child. An explanation can come later, when the rule is no longer being broken and you can give appreciation for that fact. Think about video games: Children playing these games climb to new levels all the time, encountering new rules along the way. They most optimally learn those rules through experience. By allowing them to learn your rules in the same manner, you provide them the gift of a clear experience.

In some households, there may be rules that require elucidation – that are too complex for children to learn through experience. It's okay to have a conversation about rules like these. For example: Let's say you require that your children spend at least two minutes brushing their teeth at the end of the day. It's best to spell that out (and maybe use a timer) to help children succeed in following that rule. Or perhaps you have specific requirements about how the child's room is kept or how the toys get put away; those can be specifically defined to the child.

Keep your expectations high. Focus on praising the children for rules not broken. Assume that all of your children know right from wrong in any situation, and expect that they will seek guidance when they are confused. Let them know that, if they are not sure why they've gotten a time-out/reset, they are free to ask once they've completed it. (Don't tell them if they don't ask!) If clarification is sought in a positive way, offer acknowledgment and praise; if it's in the form of an argument, give a reset. Clarification is best given by way of positivity, when those unclear rules are *not* being broken.

Q: My child didn't put away his iPod when I told him to. I warned him that I'd take it if he didn't do as I said, and he didn't, so I took it. The rest of the day, he was impossible. What did I do wrong?

A: This is a negativity leak. First, you gave him a warning. Then, by taking away the iPod, you showed the child that you don't trust him to manage his own impulses. He responded to your negative expectations with accelerated rule breaking.

The child's behavior is his decision. You can't stop a child from breaking rules. He earned a reset by not immediately following your direction. Stay in the moment; let the child know that he has full responsibility for his choices to follow or break the rules by issuing a consequence; issue another if needed; be unstintingly strict; and relentlessly point out the positive. Expect compliance and don't fear not getting it – or, at least, don't show that you're afraid of non-compliance.

Q: I often find myself praising all my children as a group: "You are all showing great dedication to finishing your homework," for example. Is this OK?

A: This can inadvertently energize negativity. If your praise is general and your consequences are specific, you may end up attracting the children to acting-out behaviors because that's when they are getting more of your intimate, personal energy. Do your best to be specific and personal with praise. This alone will help your children have a more differentiated and discerning sense of intelligence, and typically, a higher and more distinguished level of development. Along with a higher level of development comes a better ability to live one's life with integrity, differentiation and distinction.

Q: How can I find out what has happened between my children when I come in and find them both crying and/or hitting – without giving energy to negativity?

A: What parent hasn't stepped into this kind of scene: two or more children shouting and crying, someone's been hit, and no one seems able to stop hollering about how it was someone else's fault? Such situations can seem to spring out of nowhere and can become ferocious – even dangerous – without much warning. How do you handle this in the context of this approach?

Consider the dangers inherent in the usual approach, which would be to dig and question until you figure out who's at fault and then deliver a consequence to whichever one "started it." The moment you ask why the children are breaking rules, you're jumping into negativity with both feet. The child who is creating the most problems ends up getting the most energy. By targeting one child in the fracas, you reinforce and energize that child's choices to create pandemonium – deepening her impression that intimacy and relationship come her way through adversity.

In the purest sense of the Nurtured Heart Approach, you don't need to know why or how or whose fault it was. **You need only to stay in the moment and deal with what's in front of you.** Mining for the source of the problem only gives energy to the problem. Give time-outs/resets to everyone involved who is breaking a rule when you walk in. Then, it's back to time-in.

Asking why might well produce more attempts by the child to engage over problems. On the other hand, *assuming* why keeps the consequence clean and gives you a vantage point for energizing new related successes after the time-out is completed.

Trust your gut as to what's happened, even at the risk of being wrong. It's better to enforce a limit clearly based on a wrong assumption about who did what than to mount a CSI. Inquiries ("who started it?") and problem-oriented discussions are almost always lose-lose propositions. You're sending wrong energy and relationship out to the children at the wrong time, woven into the context of problems.

Consider allowing the children to come up with possible solutions on their own. If you let them, and if you show them that you expect them to, they will probably seek advice and find viable answers to their problems. Here's how: Once you've encountered the situation, make your assumption, reset as needed for rules broken, acknowledge successful resets, and then leave the situation open to the children. In the ensuing moments, capture in your lens anything you see as positive steps toward addressing the issue. Then, *confront that success with applause, appreciation, explanation and delight* – positive relationship!

For example: Let's say you walk in on siblings Henry and Cory as they are physically fighting. You time-out/reset them first, then say, "I want to tell you both that I appreciate your getting hold of your emotions and sitting through your time-out. That showed a lot of self-control and power." Then you can say, "It looks like you were fighting over the toy, and I assume you were trying to find a solution and it got out of control."

Cory says, "He hit me, so I got mad and hit him back," and Henry says, "He wouldn't give me my toy back, so I tried to get it and I guess I hit him." You can then say, "Cory, I see that you felt angry and that you wanted to keep playing with that toy. You are being great by talking clearly about what you were feeling. Henry, you wanted your toy back, and you did your best to wait, but lost your temper. You explained yourself clearly, too, and you can be proud of turning this around and telling the truth. And now you are both being respectful to one another and the toy is here and you are not fighting. Looks like you found at least one solution – to be respectful by waiting and listening to what the other needs. That's a great solution."

If you feel compelled to discuss "why," just know it's a slippery slope and do so only if you have the greater purpose of pointing out successes.

The Nurtured Heart Approach is All About Empowering the Child
When children feel that their ability to be loved, feel safe and enjoy life is dependent upon the (sometimes inconsistent) whims of adults, is it any wonder that they act out to try to gain a sense of control? A child who does not feel powerful is more likely to try to use whatever means he can find to manipulate his world.

Many parents have struggles with toilet training; with getting children to eat healthfully; or with getting children to wear appropriate clothing. Your child may refuse to stop playing to go to the bathroom and end up with soiled clothing that has to be washed immediately; or your child may think it's a good idea to eat cheese doodles for breakfast, lunch and dinner; or perhaps your child vociferously insists that flip-flops in the dead of winter make perfect fashion sense. It's fairly common knowledge that the child who really digs in on these fronts is in need of a sense of control and power.

Some parents mistakenly believe that giving the child more choices is the way to move her into a more compliant place; but this often backfires as the child becomes increasingly confused about the boundary between right and wrong behavior. Both children and adults can end up bewildered by too many choices.

The key to handing children a sense of power is to instill inner wealth. Show them that a wide range of appreciation is readily available to them, that they are already great and that they are capable and responsible beings (the relentless pursuit of positivity). Show them the boundaries with crisp clarity (strictness) and give them the power to step over. Show them that their power lies in their choices to *not* break rules (not energizing negativity).

Applaud healthy choices and healthy use of power and be as creative as you need to be in forging opportunities to show your appreciation. I contend that compliments like the following are by far the better way to teach about choices:

"Mary, I am so grateful that you chose to stay in this afternoon to get your homework done so you could get a good night's rest."

"Justin, I appreciate how thoughtful and considerate you were earlier in helping your sister adjust the seat of her bike. That was such a kind choice."

And I believe that the best way to teach about power is to create instances of acknowledging healthy power.

"Adam, what you did in suggesting that your friends take turns with the equipment was great leadership. It was a very wonderful way to collaborate and help everyone feel successful and have fun. That positive influence was very powerful."

"Marcus, I really appreciate how you applied yourself to your assignment. Your way of combining your thoughts and your intuition was very visionary. Those are very powerful qualities. Congratulations."

One of the beauties of this approach is that everyone gets to be powerful. The parent does not give up power and control so that the child can have it. Everyone gets to enjoy the greatness and inner wealth that is his or her birthright.

CHAPTER EIGHT

The Nurtured Heart Approach through the Life Span

You love your children. You tell them so every chance you get. You wish they could grasp the depth, width, breadt, and weight of that love – and be able to hold it inside themselves as a source of fortitude and joy. "I love you" doesn't even seem to tell the smallest part of the story.

This is exactly what the Nurtured Heart Approach is about: It is not about saying "I love you," but about *acts of love* that fill the recipient with a deep assurance that he is not only okay, but he is *great*. He is not only worthy of love when he's "being good"; his very essence is worth celebrating on a daily basis.

The child raised with this approach experiences that his worth is seen and acknowledged by his parents, the people who are most important to him and who know him better than anyone else on the planet. No leap of faith is necessary for the child to gain an inheritance of love and the gift of seeing his own beautiful essence. By his feeling appreciated he comes to appreciate himself. By his coming to see that he has importance and meaning to others, he comes to trust that he is important and meaningful.

How About You?

How about *you?* Do you love yourself? Do you see your own greatness? Can you set a shining example of self-love for your children?

The question isn't "Are you great?" and it's not "How great are you?" It's "How much greatness are you going to allow yourself to birth and experience in this lifetime?" And "How much greatness are you going to send out of yourself to others in this lifetime?"

If this sounds like a place you've never been and don't know how to go to, you aren't alone, and using this approach to support your children's inner wealth will move you in a better direction. Perhaps you are just beginning to realize your own capacity for greatness.

I've worked with hundreds of parents who have become truly extraordinary parents, despite having been raised in a way totally contrary to the Nurtured Heart Approach. You do not have to possess consistent, stunning inner wealth of your own in order to bring your children to that place. But you can improve your application of the Nurtured Heart Approach by nurturing your own inner wealth.

We've all heard that, without some level of self-love, you cannot love another. Many of us have learned, in our paths through intimate relationships and marriage, that a person who is unhappy, angry, steeped in self-hatred, or damaged by life often ends up seeking 'fixes' in another person. Thinking that this or that mate will give us what we can't give ourselves is a setup for disappointment. And sometimes, we end up trying to fill our own gaps, gain inner wealth, or work out our frustrations through our children – possibly at their expense.

Understanding this, and seeing how this approach could benefit parents as well as children, has inspired me to embark on an exploration of the use of this approach *on one's self,* in adulthood. Those of us who were not parented in this fiercely positive manner can, in essence, *re-parent ourselves* using this approach – which will, in turn, better equip us with the inner wealth to propel greatness within our children and others in our lives. The outcome will be greater joy, presence and peace in your life.

My Own Journey

Nearly 10 years ago, about the time my first book came out, I noticed my own habit of defaulting to negativity. Despite the positivity I was spouting in my workshops and writings, my tendency was to default to worry, doubt and fear – all debilitating emotions. I didn't believe then, nor do I believe now, that we are born to acquire these defaults; they are wrapped up in our culture. As a result, we experience downloads to our personal software programs that cause us to take a defensive, negative stance in the world. Often, even if we think we are highly positive, when the going gets rough, the dam of negativity can break…and then we can feel inundated with all that transpires.

One night I noticed, in startling Technicolor, that if I left my mind to its own devices and inclination, it would wander consistently and deeply into the realms of negative thought – despite knowing that it was unproductive and stress-producing and predictably left me in a compromised position.

In a blast of clarity, I saw it as a *default setting*. Our computers are set to default settings, and so are our thoughts. If this is true, I surmised, there must be a hidden pull-down menu of other possibilities – all sorts of pop-up windows and boxes to alter that default. In a heartbeat, it came to me that there's got to be an advanced setting, an equally possible and greater realm of positivity that's there for the taking…a realm that can be just as highly charged and automatic as negativity.

I began to willfully take myself on a journey of positivity. I didn't start out with greatness, but with appreciation. I used the techniques outlined in this book *on myself* in an effort to change my default settings – to de-energize negativity within myself and to energize the positive. Over time, this journey crystallized into a smaller but no less brilliant jewel: It's less about using the specific techniques or stances of the Nurtured Heart Approach than about seeing your own greatness and the greatness of others – and about shifting defaults of negativity to defaults to greatness.

I came to see fear, worry and doubt the way one might see a computer virus: a temporary glitch, not the natural state of the program, and something that simply needs to be 'firewalled' or removed. Do we have to figure out who gave us the virus to be free of it and escape its clutches? Or can we just clear out our hard drive and move forward? If your child goes from intensely challenging to intensely wonderful, do you really need to send that child to psychoanalysis in order to process the period of time during which he was challenging, or are you just fine moving on and enjoying the new glory of him being wonderful? I think you know the answer to these questions, having reached this point in the book.

Most people start out their lives curious, adventurous and fearless. It is interactions with the people in their lives – people to whom they entrust their entire beings, including their psyches – that transform them to a place where worry, depression and fear are constant companions. This is no one's fault; parents and other influential adults do the best they can with the tools and resources they have. As you have already discovered in reading this book, even innocent and well-intentioned conventional styles of parenting can inadvertently contribute to setting the default to negativity.

You are doing your part to break this cycle by cultivating inner wealth in your children using some new tools. Now it's time to tend to your own garden – or, going back to the computer metaphor, to loosen the grip of those pesky viruses on your hard drive and give yourself some great new software in the form of living in your own greatness.

Many people are driven to "do the right thing" out of fear that's powered by religion (i.e., fear of 'fire and brimstone'). Doing right for reasons other than your own eventually incurs its own price: When the motive is fear, people become divided and the seeds of conflict are sown. Doing right out of one's desire to fulfill the purpose of greatness is an expression and experience of the love that drives the universe. Why not make that choice? Most religions, at their core, are about love: God's love and people's desire to love one another and themselves.

Be Your Own Therapist

For nearly half a century, psychotherapy has been the standard intervention for those of us who are having difficulty coping with life, relating with others and being happy. As a psychotherapist myself, I don't wish to denigrate this field; it has helped a lot of people. But today, there are so many psychotherapeutic approaches and so many practitioners to choose from that it can be hard to find the right fit. One can easily waste months or years (and a good amount of money) with the wrong therapist or the wrong approach.

All of that might just become unnecessary if you viewed the concepts introduced in these pages in the spirit of being your own therapist. You could – as Puran Bair, a contributor to this book's Foreword, said to me one day – "blast depression [or anxiety, or addictions, or self-esteem issues] away with greatness." You can get in touch with your own perfection and choose to shine a light there. Might this be the key to a spiritual awakening and to a state of peaceful happiness? Could it be a cure for depression?

I don't yet know, but all evidence suggests that the current interventions to "treat" depression as a mental illness are just another version of throwing $100 bills at negativity. Dwelling on the problems and on the past that created those problems may eventually bring one to a place of understanding from which to step out of self-destructive patterns. The risk of this path is that it becomes yet another way of heightening the internal programming that tells us that *much more relationship, internal connection and intimacy are available through adversity.* And understanding alone, though highly valuable, does not guarantee a new sense of greatness.

But dwelling directly on your own greatness and successes – building your own inner wealth – is a much more streamlined path to that place.

When you were a child, you relied upon the help and support of adults to give you the tools for life; as an adult, you have the wisdom and power to help and support yourself. You can use the Nurtured Heart Approach to do this. Whether you choose to see it as re-parenting or self-therapy, engaging in this process will bring you to a level of happiness and confidence likely to positively alter the course of your life, your work and your relationships. And it is a process that does not require anyone else's participation.

My next book will address this spiritual process of infusing the self with inner wealth. Here, my intention is to give you a preview of how the underlying concepts of the Nurtured Heart Approach are relevant to adults like you.

Transforming Drama

The adult version of attraction to negativity manifests in the way many of us create drama in our lives. Most of us don't even realize we're doing it. Consider for yourself: Do you ever start a fight with your spouse to get that rush of a good argument? Do you make choices in your life to gossip or do things that might be hurtful to others, when you don't really need to make those choices? Or do others in your life seem to do this?

One thing is certain: Excitement usually transpires in the wake of it, and although it might be painful, it can be quite energizing.

Adults in Westernized cultures tend to be drawn to drama in all of its permutations: on television, in books and interpersonally. Our attraction to violence comes from this fascination with drama – the more intense, the better. Adults who are drawn to positivity and inner wealth may even be scorned by others as boring. A positive outlook can even be regarded as "childish," an adjective typically used to infer naïveté or lack of mature intelligence and not all of the wonderful qualities children possess.

It seems that the magnetism that drama has for us is part of our wiring. After all, we humans have been telling dramatic tales since prehistory. In a sense, we seem to require drama. When we are exhilarated and invigorated by drama, we are swept into the moment, alert and awake.

We want ecstatic experience; we crave catharsis; we long for that rush of endorphins that comes from the experience of drama and its resolution. The key, in my approach, is *to create drama around greatness and positivity.*

In my approach, I purposefully use dramatic language – *hijacking* the child into success; *confronting* the child with her greatness; *annihilating* his old negative self with evidence of greatness; *igniting* greatness in children; the *fierce* and *relentless* pursuit of positivity; *accusing* someone of being great; *taking a warrior-like stance.* It's an effort to infuse the approach with the drama that we so clearly yearn for. It's a way of transforming this natural human attraction into a positive realm.

As I continue to refine and shape the approach itself and my ways of teaching it to others, I continue to search for colorful ways to describe this drama of greatness. I seek out language that excites others (and myself) to new levels of aliveness. As you join me on this path, notice those moments when you are being motivated by an attraction to drama or a need to create drama to have that feeling of internal connection and aliveness. Notice how the drama that comes almost automatically in our internal dialogues concerns worries, fears and doubts. Recognize that you're really after the energy, and that you can choose to put it somewhere else.

In the Nurtured Heart Approach, we do not try to get rid of the energy and negative drama; instead, we *transform it.* We channel and redirect it to the positive. To flourish and to help our children do the same, we do not have to deny the basic thrust of human feelings and thoughts – we simply transform them. We utilize the exact same energy to provide thrust to the new realm of greatness – to propel inner wealth.

Will anyone be harmed when you gift yourself with messages that you possess the greatness of wisdom, courage, and compassion? Who would be upset if, in your internal dialogue, you appreciated your moments of embodying the great qualities of integrity and honor, helpfulness and creativity? Will it ruin your day? Will it ruin anyone's day?

How to Begin to Embrace and Cultivate Your Own Greatness

Even if you don't play golf or watch TV, you certainly know who Tiger Woods and Oprah Winfrey are. Both serve as models of greatness to countless people.

If you ever see Tiger setting up a shot, you see that he envisions it clearly before he hits the ball. He knows where that ball needs to go, and nine times out of 10, he seems to put it there. Oprah has an amazing gift for envisioning ways of making the world a better place – and manifesting her vision. Envisioning your own greatness is all that's necessary to make it real and actuate its huge energy. You are the conjurer. You call up that greatness by putting your energy there and envisioning it.

You can invoke your own greatness simply by saying to yourself, "Here is a quality of my greatness that I can see right now," whenever you think of it. You can acknowledge that quality as it is revealed in this moment, or you can look at a past expression of that greatness. Make the acknowledgement as irrefutable as possible, based on actual evidence. However, you can cultivate a miracle of greatness from a molecule by breathing life into even a small hint of a quality you wish to enhance.

For example: perseverance is a quality that I would like to cultivate. Right now, I am persevering on a project despite wavering energy. I can observe this tiny molecule of perseverance in myself as evidence that I do, in fact, embody this great quality. I can breathe life into its enhancement by "accusing" myself of *being the greatness of perseverance*, right now. And from that point of view of capturing it in my lens, the truth is that I do possess that quality of greatness. The intentions relayed in the stories of Shamu and the toll-taker have helped me enormously in this regard.

You don't have to worry about going into precise detail when recognizing your own qualities of greatness; you can use a sort of "shorthand" version of the Nurtured Heart Approach – you know and recognize all the details in your own mind without having to elucidate them.

For example:

"A quality of greatness I have is humor, and I know that because I made my son laugh at my funny faces this morning."

"A quality of greatness I have is that I'm loving, and I sense that because I am sitting next to my spouse and giving him all of my attention and care."

"A quality of greatness I have is creativity, and I know that because I am figuring out a great new filing system here at the office."

From there, as you begin to believe it, you can shorthand it even more:

"I am great humor."

"I am great love."

"I am great creativity."

Words have such power in the human consciousness!

Then, experiment with even more advanced acknowledgements of greatness:

"I am the greatness of love."

"I am the greatness of laughter."

"I am the greatness of humor."

"I am the greatness of creativity."

"I am the greatness of beauty."

"I am the greatness of compassion."

If you find yourself at a loss as to what to say, you can get your momentum going by simply thinking or saying, "I am great," or "I am greatness" over and over and over. Or even "I am."

Other ideas: "I am the greatness of…"

Being a warrior (the positive side of power)

Greatness (sure – why not?)

Fearlessness

Service

Discernment

Giving

Receiving

Helpfulness

Grace

Laughter

Inspiration

Encouragement

Support

Brilliance

Intelligence

Focus

Motivation

Illumination

Light

Patience

Enlightenment

Attunement

Strength

Determination

Generosity

Magnanimity

Courage

Wisdom

Charisma

Sensuality

Artistry

Sexuality

Intuition

Foresight

Responsiveness

Action

Power

Judgment

Thoughtfulness

Consideration

Differentiation

Consciousness

Forgiveness

Outrage (righteous indignation)

Activism

Conscientiousness

Wakefulness

Clarity

Meaningfulness

Perspective

Calmness

Rectitude

Fortitude

Perseverance

Lovingness

Principle

Playfulness

Plasticity

Purpose

Grace

Appreciativeness

Effort

Fascination

Enjoyment

Energy

Connection

Relationship/friendship

Intimacy

Cheerfulness

Longing for/remembering God

Belonging

Community-mindedness

Mindfulness

Opportunism

Refusal/opposition

Daring

Being in the now

Positivity

Organization

Being extraordinary

Activeness

Nimbleness

Protectiveness

Brazenness

Loveliness

Lovingness

Valor

Togetherness

With these reflections, begin to focus on your breath. A deep intake and full exhale of breath moves the energy (prana) through your body like nothing else. Wring the last bit of breath from the depth of your belly and feel the stale prana moving out. With the intake, feel greatness flowing in. Allow the voice you give to your reflections to arise not from your head, but from your heart. Time them with the rhythm of your heart and experience its expansion.

Puran and Susannah, the authors of the Foreword, have done amazing work in the understanding and teaching of heart-centered breath work, and I have found it to be highly valuable in my work to cultivate my own inner wealth. Coordinating the breath with the heartbeat and visualizing those two rivers synergistically carrying messages of greatness to self and others is extremely powerful. (Please refer to the Resources section for the titles of their books and contact information for their heart-rhythm meditation workshops.)

I used to be afraid that people or circumstances might abrade my courage, will, power or light, but this changed once I realized that no one but me is in charge of my spirit and my greatness. If a voice comes up to counter these observations of greatness, simply give yourself a reset and head for the next positive moment. Just as The Nurtured Heart Approach is used externally in parenting, take a stand and refuse to give internal energy and relationship to negativity – yours or that of others.

This is not about hubris, vanity or an over-inflated version of yourself. It is about choosing to see in yourself the greatness that already resides there. As with igniting the greatness within your child, you can start by noticing and appreciating tiny instances of any aspect of greatness that surface in yourself.

For example: At the moment, as I sit here writing these words, I am doing my best to explain this concept in a way that will help readers take the ball and run with it. If I wanted to stop for a moment and be appreciative, I could say: *I see the greatness of my caring and compassion.*

My point is this: Shining even a little light on any quality can be like dropping a match in the forest on a high-danger day. It can ignite a presence of greatness that might just have a life of its own. It just might create a blaze of greatness. Of course, the best way to help it take off is to shine this light of greatness on as many aspects as possible of the "whole you" in the course of your day.

And I have come to feel, by way of my own experiment in applying this to myself, that this is the best kind of blaze. At this point, I don't see the down side of taking this path. On my deathbed, I don't believe that I will have any of the kind of regrets that come from a life unlived.

In my own journey, choosing to blaze this path of my own greatness has clearly led me into more interesting and illuminating levels of seeing and appreciating the greatness in others. I cannot help but feel the link.

Seeing yourself in the light of greatness is a great gift. Once you take this path, you may never want to turn back. **Gratefulness = greatfulness = great-fullness**…loving ourselves as we wish to love others and as we wish to love God. Whom does that hurt?

Trust that, as you find pieces of your greatness, it opens up with ease, like a flower that's been wanting to bloom for the longest time.

You can multiply the impact of building your internal greatness by imagining that you're shouting it on the inside, as though from a rooftop. Think of Tiger Woods saying "YES!" after a great shot. Perfect drama.

Choose to assume and attribute greatness. Choose to sense that a little bit of greatness is evidence that much more exists, like the tip of an iceberg barely revealing the massiveness of itself beneath the surface. Choose to believe that there are always greater levels of greatness and that *you are already embodying them.* As Meister Eckert said: "A seed of God grows into God – so let yourself go."

To Your Greatness,

Howard Glasser, M.A.

RESOURCES

Books on the Nurtured Heart Approach

Those listed below are available in most libraries, bookstores and online sources. They can also be ordered at the Nurtured Heart Approach websites, www.difficultchild.com or www.nurturinggreatness. net, or with a toll free call to 800-311-3132.

- *Transforming the Difficult Child, The Nurtured Heart Approach* (1999) by Howard Glasser and Jennifer Easley.
- *101 Reasons to Avoid Ritalin Like the Plague AND One Great Reason Why It's Almost ALWAYS Unnecessary* (2005) by Howard Glasser with Melissa Lynn Block.
- *The Inner Wealth Initiative – The Nurtured Heart Approach for Educators* (2007) by Howard Glasser and Tom Grove with Melissa Lynn Block.
- *Transforming the Difficult Child Workbook – An Interactive Guide to the Nurtured Heart Approach* (2008) by Howard Glasser, Joann Bowdidge and Lisa Bravo.

Audio-Visual Resources
Transforming the Difficult Child – The Nurtured Heart Approach Training tapes are available on CD (audio only, 2.5 hours); on audiotape (audio only, 2.5 hours); on VHS (audio-visual, 2.5 hours); and on DVD (audio-visual, with a six-hour version and a four-hour version)

Nurtured Heart Approach support information:
Two websites are available to those who seek further information about the Nurtured Heart Approach: www.difficultchild.com or www.nurturinggreatness.net. Both have these additional features:

- Research findings related to this work
- Information about coaching and therapy services
- Information about ongoing workshops and Advanced Trainings
- Information about creating training events for your organization
- An online discussion forum
- An online store that carries related products

Books on Heart Rhythm Meditation:

- *Living From the Heart: Heart Rhythm Meditation* (1998) by Puran Bair.
- *Energize Your Heart: In 4 Dimensions* (2007) by Puran and Susanna Bair.

Heart Rhythm Meditation support information:
There is a website supporting Heart Rhythm Meditation: http://www. appliedmeditation.org/Heart_Rhythm_Meditation/meditation.shtml as well as further information on The Institute for Applied Meditation and its programs at: http://www.appliedmeditation.org/. Puran and Susanna Bair can also be reached at 520-299-2170.